interspersed throughout are helpful stories which themselves teach and illustrate. Throughout the book, Houston points us to Jesus, suggesting the difference obedience to His Word would make — in all areas of life. I enjoyed it!

Dr Eugene Habecker

God often teaches us through the stories of other people and we often find it easier to learn through stories. That's why there are so many of them in the Bible. Tom Houston has brought his skills and experience as a seasoned Bible teacher to the stories of people in the earliest church. He brings them alive. He's not afraid to use his imagination but he never does so to undermine what the Bible says. His discerning eye means he applies them aptly to today, using a wide-range of contemporary stories from the world church to drive the lessons home. The book is written with crystal-clear simplicity and is a delight to read. Not one chapter outstays its welcome. This is a rich book which is accessible to a wide readership, which I hope it gets.

Derek J Tidball
London Bible College

Characters Around the Church

Witnesses to the Birth of the Jerusalem Church

Tom Houston

Christian Focus

ISBN 1-85792-803-2

Copyright © Tom Houston 2003

Published in 2003
by
Christian Focus Publications, Ltd.
Geanies House, Fearn, Tain,
Ross-shire, IV20 1TW, Great Britain.

www.christianfocus.com

Cover design by Alister MacInnes

Printed and bound by
Cox and Wyman, Reading, Berkshire

Contents

Introduction

Introduction

This is the third in a series of books that focus on the characters in a particular period of the Bible story. Its focus is on the Jerusalem church in the first half of the Acts of the Apostles. I have called it, 'Characters around the Earliest Church' because the phrase, 'the early church' usually includes Paul and the mixed or non Jewish churches outside Palestine. Paul never really worked with the Jerusalem church and so only appears here as Saul the Persecutor. Barnabas and Agabus are also left until a later book where they more properly belong.

I have used the Jewish title 'Messiah' for Jesus and not the Greek 'Christ' to underline the debate that was really going on in this period.

This was a crucial period in the history of the church to which we return each year in the period between Easter and Pentecost. I trust that this will enable wider ranging reflection on the formative experiences of those involved.

The approach via characters is driven by the conviction that the narratives and the people in the Bible are there as examples and warnings for later generations like our own. (1 Cor.10:11) It is, therefore, not an idealized picture of the earliest church. Not only are characters outside the church examined, but the deficiencies and process of growth in the Christians are explored. The range of characters covered enables us to look at the social and political background of the events described and brings out the warmth of relations between characters in the wider fellowship. Looking at characters separately, who are involved in the same incident leads to some duplication. I have sometimes left this in so that each chapter can stand by itself.

There is some room for conjecture as to how and where events in the Acts occurred. I have not shrunk from using my imagination to suggest possible solutions to what is not in the text, always trying to remain consistent with what is said.

1

The Twelve:

Getting it together

Acts 1

Implosion

The group of men whom we call 'the glorious company of the Apostles' imploded on the evening before Good Friday. The fallout was distinctly messy and could well have signalled the end of the movement they had joined. The character fault lines that criss-crossed the surface of their group opened up simultaneously and left each of them stranded in the loneliness of their particular temperament.

Peter's self-confident and pigheaded boastfulness propelled him into denying any knowledge of Jesus, not once, or twice, but three times and the third time with a mouth-full of foul language. (Matt.26:72)

Judas's greed and sticky fingers led him to abandon the sinking ship but not before he had made a financial killing to tide him over for a while. He did not live to enjoy it. His desolation made him commit suicide. (Matt.27:5)

Thomas' cussed pessimism drove him to isolate himself from the others and sometimes stop meeting with them even to eat.

James and John's, self confessed naked ambition to have the highest places in the coming kingdom antagonizd the other ten and even began to loosen the ties between the brothers themselves (Mark 10:35-45).

We know less about the rest of the group who are not named for any particular misdemeanour. We only know they all forsook Jesus and fled (Mark 14:50).

It was a sorry state of affairs even before Jesus died, but after he was crucified, it was devastating and, to any observer, was signalling a speedy end to their enterprise.

Losing the Plot

It is clear that they were not on the same wavelength as Jesus. They had missed many clues he had given them about what he was here to do. They had managed to shut out from their comprehension even the direct statements he had made. Their Galilean/Jewish worldview had effectively shut them off from even entertaining the propositions he was making. It was not surprising then, that things came apart at the seams when confronted with all the naked power of the authorities in a city where they were strangers.

The extent of the damage that had been done was shown by the fact that when Jesus did rise from the dead, not a single one of them believed that he had or that he could. The writers go out of their way to make that clear.

The Way Back

After Jesus rose from the dead, the first phase of their rehabilitation was at the personal level. Peter, in several encounters, was won back from his disloyalty and despair – a much humbled man (Mark 16:17).

Thomas was given the evidence that his doubt demanded and recognized finally that he was dealing with a Jesus that went beyond some of the human categories he had tried to put him in (John 20:24-29).

John was singled out for special treatment that pulled him out from under the dominance of his more explosive brother (John 21:22-24).

The rest were enticed back into the comfort of the group by his appearances among them.

The motherly and feminine influence of the women who had travelled with them, both nurtured them and gave them something to push against as they came to terms with their trauma in the new day of the resurrection. All of that is indicated in the endings of the gospels (Luke24:36-49).

They had almost six weeks before Jesus ascended to his father in heaven. Some of the time was spent in Jerusalem, where they were strangers and some in Galilee, which was home. But they kept together as a group.

Intermittently, Jesus appeared to them and, by the power of the Holy Spirit, gave them new instruction in the light of his resurrection. A major theme of this new teaching was about the Kingdom of God. Another was about the Holy Spirit.

New Teaching Misunderstood

What they understood of this latest teaching, we can only surmise. They knew they had to stay in Jerusalem because they did wait. They knew that this had something to do with their receiving the Holy Spirit in a way that matched what John the Baptist did when he baptized people in the river Jordan.

We are told that they were slow to grasp what he was saying about the kingdom of God.

Towards the end of this interim, somewhat unpredictable forty days, they came to him with a question, 'Lord, will you at this time give the Kingdom back to Israel?' Clearly, they were still thinking of the Kingdom of God in political terms. This was not surprising in the highly charged atmosphere in which they had lived from day to day in fear of their lives, from both the Roman civil and the Jewish religious authorities.

In His Time

They cannot have known how near they came to getting it all wrong. But Jesus picks up their misguided question and deals with it reassuringly, first, with the time element. Although they did not and could not know the future, or the course by which they would reach it, God knows the timing, its regular rhythms and its crises. That is always a great assurance to the people of God.

Then he links together the two subjects he has been speaking about, the Spirit and the Kingdom of God. Yes, they would receive power, but not to be administrators in a local Kingdom, but to be witnesses to him, the King, locally, regionally and internationally, of the universal Kingdom of God. That was to be their role and their task (Acts 1:7-8).

The Climax

It seems that, before they had time to think,
Jesus was taken up into heaven before their
eyes and a cloud received him out of their sight.
There had been nothing like this in the
experience of most of them. Three of them,
Peter, James and John, would recall the
foretaste of this they had when Jesus was
transfigured before them on the mountain
(Mark 9:2-3). This time there was also a
commentary on what was happening. Two
men dressed in white suddenly stood beside
them and said, 'Galileans, why are you
standing there looking up at the sky? This
Jesus, who was taken from you into heaven,
will come back in the same way that you saw
him go to heaven' (Acts 1:11). They saw that
was what had happened and this was how it
would end with all of history in between.

The Incubation Period of the Early Church

There is a distinct change of mood and tempo
after this. Back they go to the city, a fifteen to
twenty minutes walk. They went to the room
where they were staying and it sounds as
though they re-constituted themselves for the
work that was to follow. There are subtle
differences from anything that had happened
earlier.

It may have been the same upper room as on the evening before Good Friday, but the tone was decidedly different. Then they had argued about who was the greatest. Now they met 'with one accord'. It is a new word only used by Luke in Acts, except for one time when Paul uses it in Romans. It describes a new reality. A group that was fractured by weakness, self-centredness and competitive spirits, is now for the first time united, of one spirit, with one motive and of great strength.

The newness of the reality is signalled by little, but significant things. It is no longer, 'Peter, Andrew, James and John ...' that head up the list of Apostles. It is, 'Peter, John, James and Andrew...' James and John seem to have abandoned their too close attachment as brothers and John is released to be Peter's number two.

This began a succession of meetings in that room to pray, presumably for the Holy Spirit in whom they were to be immersed as John baptized people in the river Jordan. But they prayed with the women included in the 'one accord' and not in separate courts as in the Temple, or on different sides of the building, as in the Synagogues.

Mary, the Mother of Jesus and his brothers are there. Jesus had placed Mary in John's care

on Good Friday and James had been given a
special visit by the risen Jesus (1 Cor. 15:7).

But there was something missing. They
were only eleven apostles. Judas was not there
and that has to be our next story.

Six Weeks to change

Before we leave this group, however, we need
to recognize that the people in the upper room,
on the evening before Good Friday, had to
tread a six week road of transformation before
they were ready to be witnesses to Jesus –
corporately or as individuals.

Six weeks is usually the time it takes to
change a habit. New Year's resolutions have
to be maintained without a break until the
middle of February if they are to hold. Can it
happen again? It will take time. It will take
honesty. It will take effort and demand action
from everyone, not just a few. But if these
things are dealt with, yes it can happen again.
Everywhere it does happen, I believe, God will
give another little Pentecost. The world will
begin again to believe that we really have good
news. When Jesus comes and changes people
and enables them to live together in peace, they
will want to know about him.

In the Church of Jesus Christ today, we
need to move from conflict to consensus, from

arguments to agreements, from fighting to friendliness, from shouting to sharing, from competing to being co-operative. We need it in our homes and in our places of work. We need to ask ourselves are we individually a force for cohesion or for fragmentation in the body of Christ.

That is my testimony, in part. I was a separatist as a young man. I participated in a divisive movement in my own denomination. I wanted everybody to believe as I did. I wanted the folk that I did not agree with to be removed. But the Lord has taken me through a few hedges backwards over the years. I have come to realize that two-way forgiveness is the essence of the gospel. I am forgiven and become forgiving. As that works day-by-day, then I become a force for cohesion and not a force for fragmentation.

Every church needs all of its people to be growing as forces for cohesion, for healing wounds, for bringing divisions to reconciliation, to help people deal with their anger and not just express it, to lowering the temperature of jealousy and envy, to try to mitigate strife. That is what we need in the church of Jesus Christ. We need to be a force for cohesion. This change can be painful.

A Modern Day Example

It was in the Melkite Church in the village of Ibillin in Galilee in Palestine in 1967. When Elias Chacour, its Abuna, or priest, was a boy in 1947, his family had been brutally dispossessed of their land and property by the Jews. Amazingly, Elias was kept without bitterness and lived by the Beatitudes through the influence of his father, a bishop in the church and teachers in Seminary. Eventually, he was sent as a temporary priest-in-charge to the Melkite church in Ibillin in 1966. He was told on arrival by the Lay Leader of the congregation that he was not wanted and he should leave without unpacking his bags. He stayed. He stayed to tackle this community torn apart by animosities and factions between the Melkites, the Greek Orthodox and the Muslims. He visited every home but every initiative he took was rebuffed for eighteen months.

Then he had a vivid dream one night as he slept in his car. In his own (abbreviated) words, 'Then I knew for the first time that I was capable of vicious, killing hatred. I had covered my hurts with Christian responses, but inside the anger had gnawed. With this sudden, startling view of myself, a familiar inner voice spoke firmly, without compromise: if you hate your brother YOU are guilty of murder.

'Now I understood. I was aware of other words being spoken. A man was dying a hideous death at the hands of His captors – a Man of Peace, who suffered unjustly, hung on a cross. Father forgive them, I repeated. And forgive me, too. In that moment, forgiveness closed the long-open gap of anger and bitterness inside me. I knew what I must do in Ibillin.

Palm Sunday

'On Palm Sunday, every bench was packed. Most of the people would not think of missing services during the Christmas and Easter seasons, coming to be comforted by familiar customs, not out of desire for true spiritual renewal. When I stood up, raising my hands to signal the start of the service, I was jolted by stark, staring faces. Looks of open hostility greeted me. The Lay Leader's faction was clustered on one side of the church, almost challenging me with their icy glares. Indifferently, those whom the Lay Leader had ostracized sat on the opposite side. I was amazed to see Abu Mouhib, the policeman, perched in the very front row with his wife and children. In each of the other three quadrants of the church, as distant from one another as possible, were his three brothers. The sisters, I could tell, felt the tension, too, for their faces were blanched. I rose and began the first hymn, certain that no one would be attracted by our pathetically dismal singing. I thought, with sadness, of the battle lines that were drawn across the aisles of that sanctuary. And nervously, I hoped that no one would notice the odd lump in the pocket beneath my vestment.

What followed was undoubtedly the stiffest service, the most unimpassioned sermon of my life. The congregation endured me indifferently, fulfilling their holiday obligation to warm the benches. But then, they did not suspect what was coming. At the close of the liturgy, everyone rose for the benediction. I lifted my hand, my stomach fluttering, and paused. It was now or never.

The Challenge

'Swiftly, I dropped my hand and strode toward the open doors at the back of the church. Every eye followed me with curiosity. I drew shut the huge double doors. From my pocket I pulled a thick chain, laced it through the handles and fastened it firmly with a padlock.

Returning to the front, I could almost feel the temperature rising. Or was it just me?

Turning to face the congregation, I took a deep breath. "Sitting in this building does not make you a Christian," I began awkwardly. My voice seemed to echo too loudly in the shocked silence.

"You are a people divided. You argue and hate each other, gossip and spread malicious lies. What do the Moslems and the unbelievers think when they see you? Surely that your religion is false. If you can't love your brother that you see, how can you say you love God who is invisible? You have allowed the body of Christ to be disgraced."

Now the shock had turned to anger. The Lay Leader trembled and seemed as though he was about to choke. Abu Mouhib, the policeman, tapped his foot angrily and turned red around the collar. In his eyes, though, I thought I detected something besides anger.

Plunging ahead, my voice rose. "For many months, I've tried to unite you. I've failed, because I'm only a man. But there is someone else who can bring you together in true unity. His name is Jesus Christ. He is the one who gives you power to forgive. So now I will be quiet and allow Him to give you that power. If you will not forgive, we will stay locked in here. You can kill each other and I'll provide your funerals gratis."

Silence hung. Tight-lipped, fists clenched, everyone glared at me as if carved from stone. I waited. With agonizing slowness, the minutes passed. Three minutes . . . five . . .ten.. . I could hear, outside, a boy coaxing his donkey up the street and the slow clop-clop of its hooves. Still no one flinched. My breathing had become shallow and I swallowed hard. Surely I've finished everything, I chastised myself, undone all these months of hard work with my. . . Then a sudden movement caught my eye.

The Break

'Someone was standing. Abu Mouhib rose and faced the congregation, his head bowed, remorse shining in his eyes. With his first words, I could scarcely believe that this was the same hard-bitten policeman who had treated me so brusquely.

"I am sorry," he faltered. All eyes were on him. "I am the worst one of all. I've hated my own brothers. Hated them so much I wanted to kill them. More than any of you I need forgiveness."

And then he turned to me. "Can you forgive me, too, Abuna?"

I was amazed! "Abuna means our father," a term of affection and respect. I had been called other things since arriving in Ibillin, but nothing so warm.

"Come here," I replied, motioning him to my side. He came, and we greeted each other with the kiss of peace. "Of course I forgive you," I said. "Now go and greet your brothers."

Before he was halfway down the aisle, his three brothers had rushed to him. They held each other in a long embrace, each one asking forgiveness of the others.

In an instant the church was a chaos of embracing and repentance. Cousins who had not spoken to each other in years, wept together openly. Women asked forgiveness for malicious gossip. Men confessed to passing damaging lies about each other. People who had ignored the sisters and myself in the streets now begged us to come to their homes. Only the Lay Leader stood quietly apart, accepting only stiffly my embrace. This second church service, a liturgy of love and reconciliation, went on for nearly a full hour.

Then, loudly, I announced: "We're not going to wait until next week to celebrate the Resurrection. Let's celebrate it now. We were dead to each other. Now we are alive again."

I began to sing. This time our voices joined as one, the words binding us together in a song of triumph: "Christ is risen from the dead. By His death He has trampled death and given life to those in the tomb."

Even then it did not end. The momentum carried us out of the church and into the streets where true Christianity belongs. For the rest of the day and far into the evening, I joined groups of believers as they went from house to house throughout Ibillin. At every door, someone had to ask forgiveness for a certain wrong. Never was forgiveness withheld. Now I knew that inner peace could be passed from man to man and woman to woman.

Gifts of food arrived daily and, amazingly, we never purchased groceries from then on, for the generosity of these humble people was to prove bottomless.' (*Blood Brothers* by Elias Chacour pp. 168-173)

The work of reconciliation has gone on from that day until this and has been seen in countless ways.

2

Matthias

The Empty Place

Acts 1:15-26

No Rehabilitation

The eleven found their way back and were regrouped with a new oneness of accord in the old upper room. There was no way back for Judas. He died before Jesus did and missed the sequel. The eleven seemed to be very aware of this. For the first item of business was a meeting to choose a replacement.

A Place to Fill

It is important neither to overestimate nor underestimate Judas Iscariot. On the night of the Last Supper, Jesus told Judas to go out and do quickly what he had to do. The Judas factor was simple. It was treachery, disloyalty to Jesus and the others, caused in his case, by greed. Notice the effect on togetherness of what Judas was and did. There is an element of surprise here.

Jesus said on the night of the Last Supper that someone was going to betray Him. They all turned around and they said, 'Lord, is it I?' They had no idea that they had someone in their midst who was so close to treachery. When Jesus sends Judas out to do quickly what he had to do, none of the others understood why he said this. They thought he had gone out to dispense money to the poor. That indicates a secrecy, a hiddenness, a lack of transparency that Judas brought into the twelve. They could think that he was out handling the money for the poor when he was out getting money for himself and in touch with people who were actually their enemies.

That is disloyalty. Never is everything on the table. The talk outside the meeting is not the same as the talk in the meeting. People are not sure where each other really is and they were not sure on the night of the Last Supper. They had no idea it was as close to treachery as it was. There can be no oneness of mind if you have disloyalty in a group.

How was the Judas factor dealt with? Drastically. Judas removed himself from the twelve. It was either that or change. He decided not to change, but go out into the night of his own remorse, expressed in suicide. Sometimes 'oneness of accord,' can only be achieved by a person going out, if they are not prepared to change.

Still, he did return the money (Matt.27:5). He was remorseful. If everyone who took a bribe returned the money, to the world or to the church, the world and the church would be very different places. Ecclesiastical crime in the year 2001 was estimated to be worth $18 billion.

What impresses me most about this story, however, is that the disciples completed the number. They realized that everyone was necessary. Eleven was not enough. They chose a successor to Judas. They could do without Judas' treachery. They could do without Judas' greed, but they could not do without what Judas had positively. So, they elected another, someone who had been with them from the baptism of John until that moment, someone who was a witness of the resurrection. They could not do it as eleven. They had to be twelve to do it. We can do without the divisiveness in peoples' lives but we lose a lot more than their fault when a person leaves. Fragmentation, slackness in attendance, individualism are at the heart of oneness. Yet, the people who have these faults are necessary. All of our positive qualities are needed for the wholeness of the body, that we may function well.

A Procedure to Follow

Having established that they had justification for what they were doing, they used a procedure that is unique in the Bible.

They called the congregation together

The Apostles chose to call together the whole company of believers to help them decide who should replace Judas (Acts 1:15). The congregation was to be involved, but it was not just a democratic vote that decided the matter. There were other factors controlling how they went about this.

They turned to scripture

They found analogies in the experience of David as expressed in some Psalms that the Holy Spirit used to help them to understand what Jesus had suffered and what they should do about it. Although Judas had been one of the chosen group of twelve, he had forfeited his place and they needed to choose someone to take his place (Acts 1:17-20).

They stated the qualifications required

'Someone must join us as a witness to the resurrection of the Lord Jesus. He must be one of the men who were in our group during the whole time that the Lord Jesus travelled about with us, beginning from the time John preached his message of baptism until the day Jesus was taken up from us to heaven.' This was the part the congregation played. They heard the qualifications and then discussed and decided that there were two men who qualified. 'So they proposed two men: Joseph, and Matthias'.

They prayed

We have the sense that these ten days were filled with an atmosphere of deep prayer and waiting on God. This practical matter was not exempt. 'They prayed "Lord, you know the thoughts of everyone, so show us which of these two you have chosen to serve as an apostle in the place of Judas, who left to go to the place where he belongs"' (Acts 1:24).

They drew lots

This is unusual but not surprising. The lot was reverted to on a number of occasions in the Old Testament and a proverb said, 'The lot is cast in the lap, but its every decision is from the Lord' (Prov. 16:33). So, 'They drew lots to choose between the two men, and the one chosen was Matthias, who was added to the group of eleven apostles' (Acts 1:26). That this happened only once is not surprising either, for it was before the Holy Spirit had been given in Pentecostal measure. Thereafter it is the Spirit who guides their decisions.

A Person to Emulate

Although we never hear about Matthias again, there are things that we can infer from this story.

He had undergone a thorough conversion. He had been prepared for following Jesus by the stern preaching of John the Baptist. Matthias is there in the background when John tells people about the evidence of repentance; the sharing of food and clothing with those who lacked them; refraining from any form of exploitation, and contentment with one's wages. All these qualities were needed in someone who was to fill the shoes of Judas who had forgotten some of them.

Matthias heard John pointing to Jesus and saying, 'Behold the Lamb of God who takes away the sin of the world' and he had followed him faithfully for three years until he saw it happen on the cross. He had also been there when Jesus chose the twelve to be his inner band. He had been passed over, yet he accepted the fact and continued as a faithful disciple. How galling it must have been if he had in fact some inkling of suspicion about how much

Judas could be trusted, if he saw him chosen and himself passed over.

But Matthias, for all that, did not let his heart turn sour. He accepted being set aside as his proper place. No doubt, he found in himself only too many reasons why he was so set aside. He was like the defeated candidate in 'Plutarch's Lives' who, departing home from the election to his house, said to them at home that it did him good to see that there were three hundred men in Athens who were better men than he was.

Matthias had also been there when Peter kept showing off, when James and John demonstrated their censoriousness, when Thomas vented his pessimism and when all the apostles took turns in asserting that they were the best. Yet he did not call them hypocrites and walk off the scene. No, 'he companied with them all the time that Jesus went out and in among them.' (Acts 1:21 AV)

There were times when people deserted Jesus (John 6:66) but Matthias was not among them. He stayed loyal. His language would have been different from Peter's on that occasion. He would have said, 'Office or no office, election or rejection, call or no call, to whom else can I go? You have the words of eternal life.' Our reaction when we are passed over for promotion is a great test of our character.

It is to Matthias's credit that not just the other apostles but a majority, if not all, of the 120 believers present, had this same opinion of his humility and dependability.

Not only so, but Matthias had also been a witness with the eleven of the resurrection of the Lord. And these, added Peter, are the two indispensable tests of fitness for this vacant office; a three years' conversion and faithful discipleship, and also, he had seen the risen Lord with his own eyes. And the lot fell upon Matthias.

He did not go on to write a gospel although one is falsely attributed to him. He did not write letters to the churches that have been preserved for us. He must have preached, but we hear nothing of his message. He is said by tradition to have preached in Ethiopia. He was named only once and that for the qualities they were looking for in an apostle.

A Role Model

My own version of a Matthias in my lifetime is a supply preacher who used to come occasionally to preach in our local church. Andrew Broadley had a remarkable conversion on a night when he was on the way to commit suicide. His conversion so affected him that he used to stay up all night studying the Bible to make up for lost time. He used to say that he had stayed up all night doing extra night shift work in the shipyard to get extra money for drink, why should he not do as much in his following Jesus in the study of his word. He would have loved to be ordained a minister but circumstances made it impossible. He was not embittered by his disappointment. He served as he was able. He was one of the most insightful and helpful preachers I recall from my youth.

It is important to recognize the importance of all these qualifications. A thorough conversion that showed evidence of true repentance is where the genuine Christian life starts. Faithful perseverance in the face of being overlooked and wounded in other ways is how it goes on. Being absolutely convinced about the fact that Jesus rose from the dead is the key to being an effective witness and a leader among Christians.

3

Peter

Stung into Preaching

Acts 2:1-47

Peter stepped on to a track of personal development when he first encountered Jesus. He began to move from the 'Simon' that his family had made him to the 'Peter' Jesus said he could become (John 1:42). Many incidents in the four gospels record Peter's erratic progress on that development track. His major crisis had been his denial of Jesus before the crucifixion and his restoration after it. He shows he still has some prominence after the Ascension, as he presides over the election of Matthias to replace Judas.

Waiting

He was now on the edge of his most significant experience ever. We do not know what precisely he was expecting in the ten days between the Ascension and Pentecost. In

general terms, we know that he and the others
were expecting the fulfilment of a promise that
Jesus made to them that they would receive
the Holy Spirit. It would bring them unusual
power and this would equip them to be
witnesses to Jesus. There was no hint of when
or where this would happen, except that it
would be in Jerusalem (Acts 1:4). The picture
they had was that they would be 'baptised' in
the Holy Spirit and this was in some way
parallel to what John the Baptist did with
people when he 'baptised' them in the water
of the river Jordan (Acts 1:4-8). They waited
by convening regularly for prayer either in the
large room that was at their disposal or in
certain secluded areas of the very large Temple
precincts, or their homes.

Pentecost

As they waited, the time came for the joyful
feast of Pentecost or Harvest. Visitors started
crowding into the city from all over the
country, with their harvest safely gathered in.
They came also from all parts of the world. It
appears that the believers mixed with these
crowds both in the streets and in the Temple
area.

On the day before Pentecost, as evening and
night drew on, the blasts of the priests'

trumpets announced the commencement of the feast. Already in the first watch of the night, the great altar was cleansed. Immediately after midnight the Temple gates were thrown open. For, before the morning sacrifice, all the burnt and peace offerings which the people proposed to bring to the feast had to be examined by the officiating priests. It was a busy time and continued until the moment in the dawn of the day when the regular morning sacrifice was made. After that the people brought their Pentecost festive offerings as prescribed.

As they did so, the Levites were chanting the Praise Psalms to the accompaniment of a single flute. The round ringing treble of selected voices from the children of Levites, who stood on a step below their singing fathers gave richness and melody to the hymn while the people made their responses.

We do not know how far the group of waiting believers was from this central drama at the high altar. We have to imagine that it was sometime around dawn that their big day arrived. They heard the sound of rushing wind. They saw the forked tongues of fire touch the head of each person. They were all 'filled with the Holy Spirit' and began to speak out in other languages the great things that God had done.

Their urge to engage in exuberant, ecstatic witness drove them out into the open Temple areas. They attracted the attention of the very cosmopolitan crowd with increasing excitement as each heard someone's witness in the adopted language of their place of exile, although the speakers were all from Galilee.

Naturally, serious people began to ask, 'What does this mean?' Others just thought it was a huge joke and said, 'These people are drunk!' (Acts 2:1-13)

Objecting

Up to this point, none of the believers played any distinctive role. They were all filled. They all spoke with the new tongues. But, when someone suggested that they were drunk, that stung Peter into action. He was their natural spokesperson. He could not tolerate their sacred experience of an astonishing outpouring of the love of God into their hearts, being written off as some drunken orgy. He stood up and got the other eleven apostles around him where they could be seen and began to address the crowds that were running in droves to witness what was happening. He addressed both the locals and the visitors. He nips in the bud the idea that they were drunk and gives away the time of day. It was only nine o'clock in the morning. It was too early for them to be drunk.

Explaining

If they were not drunk, what was going on? An explanation was needed and Peter began to give it. In a loud voice he told them that it was the fulfilment of an old prophecy given by their prophet, Joel, centuries before. There had been acute drought and famine afflicting the whole country. The prayers of the people for rain were desperate. The prophet assured them that God would give them regular pouring rain (Joel 2:23). They would have great harvests to bring in to supply great Pentecost or Harvest Festivals. And God did send rain, but he did not stop there. They had other needs. There was also a spiritual famine for which they needed God to intervene with a similar deluge of his Spirit. Joel promised that God would do this, but did not specify the time.

Peter said the time was now. He was prompted, no doubt, by the teaching Jesus had recently given them about the parts of the Scriptures that referred to himself and his kingdom (Luke 24:27,32,45, Acts 1:3). What they were witnessing there in that small group in the Temple was the fulfilment of what the prophet, Joel had prophesied. The evidence of this spiritual deluge was there before their eyes, all these people, young men and women, older men and women, masters and lowly servants were proclaiming the message about the great things that God had done in languages they had no reason to know. But what things were these?

Accusing

He uses another statement from Joel to make the transition to his answer to the question, 'What things?' Joel had said, 'I will perform miracles in the sky above and wonders on the earth below. There will be blood, fire, and thick smoke; the sun will be darkened, and the moon will turn red as blood, before the great and glorious Day of the Lord comes.' Peter seemed to be recalling the unnatural darkness and the earthquake that was experienced when Jesus was crucified fifty days before (Matt. 27:45, 51-54), for he goes straight on to make the first ever public statement that God had raised Jesus from death. He began with what they all knew.

'Jesus of Nazareth was a man whose divine authority was clearly proven to you by all the miracles and wonders which God performed through him. You yourselves know this, for it happened here among you.' He boldly accused them, twice and unequivocally, of killing Jesus. (Acts 2:23,36) But he surprised them by a totally unexpected announcement. 'In accordance with his own plan God had already decided that Jesus would be handed over to you; and you killed him by letting sinful men crucify him.' This was a new angle on the Cross and from it he moved on to the next thing God did. 'God raised him from death, setting him free from its power, because it was impossible that death should hold him prisoner.'

Announcing

It is impossible to exaggerate the shock that this statement of Peter's would have been to its original hearers. To say that God raised him from death was a bombshell but to say that it was impossible that death should hold him prisoner must have seemed crazy. So, how did Peter argue this one. He brings out another of their Scriptures, this time from a psalm of their greatest king, David (Psa. 16:8-11). David spoke about the coming Messiah who would die and be rescued from death and Peter concluded, 'God has raised this very Jesus from death, and we are all witnesses to this fact.' The 'we' in this case was not the crowd but Peter and the

company of believers who were with him.
They had witnessed the resurrection and were
now going public about it.

The next question must have been, 'So
where is Jesus now? Produce him!' Peter
answered before it was asked. He reported the
Ascension. 'He has been raised to the right-
hand side of God, his Father, and has received
from him the Holy Spirit, as he had promised.
What you now see and hear is his gift that he
has poured out on us from heaven.' He backs
it up by another statement from David in
Psalm 110:1. For it was not David who went
up into heaven; rather he said: 'The Lord said
to my Lord: Sit here at my right until I put
your enemies as a footstool under your feet.'
His grand conclusion is, 'All the people of
Israel, then, are to know for sure that this Jesus,
whom you crucified, is the one that God has
made Lord and Messiah!' Their dream and
prayer of centuries was being fulfilled. Messiah
had come. This was Peter's second bombshell.
Jesus was their Messiah.

Reacting

'When the people heard this, they were deeply
troubled. It appears that they were convinced
by what Peter was saying about the
resurrection and Jesus being the Messiah. They

asked Peter and the other apostles, 'What shall we do, brothers?' Here we reach the most unexpected response of all. Peter did not ask for the impeachment of their rulers, or that they should make representations to Rome that Pilate should be recalled from his post. He did not thunder on about how fickle the crowd had been. Instead, he said that each person needed to repent of this sin of killing Jesus and turn away from all their sins and be baptized. God would forgive them their sins and they would receive God's gift of the Holy Spirit like the believers around him. He said it in more than one way, but it boiled down to, 'Save yourselves from the punishment coming on this wicked people!' Three thousand of them did so. If that was 10 per cent of them that would mean they had a crowd of 30,000 gathered there in the Temple area. We need to register some things about this 'new' Peter.

His Boldness

There is no doubt that Peter accused the people and their leaders in broad daylight, of what amounted to judicial murder. It was a bold thing to do. He minced no words. It is in marked contrast to the save-my-skin attitude he showed when he denied all knowledge of Jesus to a servant girl in the High Priest's palace before the crucifixion (Luke 22:54-60). He maintains this stance and, later, even goes to prison for his persistence (Acts 4:3). The Holy Spirit freed him from fear and made him ready to speak out without hesitation about what the people had done, regardless of the consequences.

His Message of Mercy

He was not vindictive. He was not out to undo what had been done. He was not on a justice crusade. He had seen his own cowardly part in getting Jesus crucified, and had been forgiven and reinstated by the risen Jesus. There was no hypocritical anger in him waiting to be expressed in trying to get his own back. No, he preached forgiveness and the possibility of change by the power of the newly poured out Spirit. He and the others had received the power to forgive, perhaps the greatest blessing of Pentecost.

Bishop Festo Kivengere of Uganda attended a great meeting of some 11,000 people in Kenya in 1958. Most of them were Christians, but there were some who had come as spectators. It was not long after hundreds of African Christians had died at the hands of the Mau Mau terrorists because they witnessed for the Lord. They died gloriously; some of them were just girls; some were young men and women; some were older. As the grace of God was being preached in this great meeting, the Spirit of God was making people respond. People were weeping.

A man stood up, absolutely overcome. He was a tough fellow, a Kikuyu by tribe, a taxi driver in the city of Nairobi. He was not the emotional type, but he was shaking from head to foot, weeping. He said, 'I am much more than a beast of a man. I have been a terrorist for the last three years. I have murdered more than sixty people. And yet somehow I feel the love of God has received me.' He began to weep again and all the people bowed their heads in prayer.

'I never expected God to receive me,' he went on. Now I know he has done so. But there may be a woman in this crowd whose husband I helped to hang in the bedroom in front of her. Can such a woman forgive such a beast of a man?' And to be sure, she was there. She stood up and walked quietly from where she was to where the man who murdered her husband was standing. Every head was bowed; no one knew what was going to happen. Then this woman stretched out her hand and put it in the hand of the man who murdered her husband, saying, 'I forgave you that night, when my husband prayed for you. You are now my brother!'

The taxi driver became an evangelist. When he speaks about the love of God, he weeps; you can't blame him! He thinks it extraordinary love which could forgive such a character and change him into a man of God and a Christian.

On the day of Pentecost, it was also the surprise of the people that Peter preached forgiveness from God, that drew them to respond to his challenge to repent and receive the Holy Spirit.

His Knowledge of Scripture

Neither Peter or any of the Apostles, in the gospels, ever quote from the OT Scriptures. Those who quote Scripture are the gospel writers, Jesus and his enemies like the Sadducees and the Pharisees. The only time Scripture is even breathed by the apostles is the question about what Malachi said about Elijah coming again (Matt. 17:10).

Peter was not a rabbi and did not come from a priestly family. He was just a rude, rather crude fisherman who would hear the Scriptures read when he attended the Synagogue on the Sabbaths. Now and later he is responsible for an avalanche of Scripture quotations, always used in a very cogent way. Jesus must have given them a very effective crash course on what scripture said about himself in the six weeks between the Resurrection and the Ascension (Luke 24:27,32,44, Acts 1:3).

From his Pentecostal experience, right to the end of his life in martyrdom, his boldness, his merciful attitude, and his Scriptural preaching and writing remained characteristic of the man. Such is the difference that the Holy Spirit makes.

4

The Lame Man

Asking for the right thing

Acts 3:1-10

The First Outsider

The first outsider that we meet around the
Jerusalem church is a lame beggar at one of
the gates of Herod's great temple. We know
he was an outsider because he was a beggar. If
he had been one of the believers, his needs
would already have been taken care of within
the new young community: 'All the believers
continued together in close fellowship and
shared their belongings with one another.
They would sell their property and possessions,
and distribute the money among all, according
to what each one needed' (Acts 2:45,46). There
was no one in the group who was in need.

An Idyllic Society?

This is a fascinating development. The apostles
themselves had sold everything and given to

the poor when they became disciples of Jesus. There were some monied women with them who provided for some of their necessities (Luke 8:1-4). More recently some wealthier men had emerged, like Nicodemus and Joseph of Arimathea, who financed the short-lived burial of Jesus. So, among the 120 who waited for the coming of the Spirit, there were people with means and people with no means.

When the 3,000 were converted after Peter's speech, it became immediately clear that there were people with property and people in abject need from the back streets and the slums of the city. The leadership did not hesitate to include in the teaching of the new believers that they should share their material possessions, to make sure there was not a needy person among them (Acts 4:34). The wealthy realized property to supply the common purse. They were in and out of each others houses, enjoying meals together in a very happy atmosphere. Prayer and praise seemed to be their natural environment. It reads like the makings of an idyllic society and it appears that they were favourably regarded by people generally. This would be weeks rather than months after Pentecost (Acts 2:46-47).

'Bliss was it in that dawn to be alive; But to be young was very heaven.'

No Money

The Lame man, as we have said, was apparently not one of their number or he would have been taken care of. He was more than forty years old (Acts 4:22) and had been lame from birth (Acts 3:2). Every day some friends carried him and deposited him at a gate of the temple to beg for money from the people who were going into the temple. No doubt they came back to take him to where he slept at night and received some share of his takings for the day.

On this particular day, about 3 o'clock in the afternoon the cripple caught sight of Peter and John going into the temple. It would appear that he knew who they were. We know they had been frequent visitors to the temple in recent days (Acts 2:46). The lame man no doubt had heard about the strange events on the first day of the Pentecost feast and the speech Peter made in explanation. We can reasonably assume that rumours would have reached him about the new and growing community that was forming among the new believers and the sharing that was taking place between the poorer and the better off.

So, for our man, here was a great chance to ask two men for a contribution who were known to be part of a new and generous community. He raised his voice and asked alms expectantly. They stopped and looked him in the eye and Peter said, 'Look at us!' He had their attention, so he looked them in the eye, really hoping to receive something.

The next words must have been a big disappointment. Peter said, 'I have no money.' How often he must have heard that excuse that made his heart sick. It is one way some people handle the problem of beggars on the streets. They leave their purse or wallet at home and then can push away the begging bowl or tin in a smug way by saying, 'I'm sorry, but I don't have any money with me.' The lame man was ready to slink back to watching the rest of the crowd, making its way through the gate, when he noticed that Peter was still talking, 'but I give you what I have. In the name of Jesus, the Messiah from Nazareth, get up and walk'

No Alms

What are we to make of the fact that Peter and John had no money? This had probably been true for years since they left everything and followed Jesus (Luke 5:11). It had become more acutely true in the days immediately before this incident because of the influx of needy people into their new and growing community. It seems that their needs were being supplied out of a common purse, back at base.

It is consistent with other interesting facts. Neither Jesus in the gospels, or any of his apostles in the Acts are ever recorded as giving money to a beggar. There was a blind beggar in the gospel of John (9:11) and another called Bartimaeus in Mark. Both received their sight but no money (10:46-52). Bartimaeus was given a chance to change his request for money and asked to receive his sight. One beggar is mentioned in one parable and Jesus has a little teaching on almsgiving in the Sermon on the mount (Matt. 6:2-4). Jesus says more about the poor. Luke reports Jesus as speaking about the poor seven times, but only twice about giving to the poor. In the Acts, he does not use the word 'poor' at all. His word in Acts is the 'needy' and then only twice (Acts 2:45, 4:34).

Poverty and Disability

So, what was this man's need? He thought it was money, so he asked for some. Peter and John looked deeper. They saw the link between his poverty and his disability and said, 'in the name of Jesus the Messiah from Nazareth, I order you to get up and walk.'

How did the lame man hear these totally unexpected words. Let me guess! This Jerusalem man would have heard of the placard that was placed above the head of Jesus on the cross two and some months ago. It read, 'Jesus of Nazareth, King of the Jews' (John 19:19). He could also have heard that Peter had said in his speech at Pentecost that by raising him from the dead God had made Jesus of Nazareth both Lord and Messiah (Acts 2:22,32,36). Now he was hearing a word of overwhelming authority telling him to get up and walk – 'in the name of Jesus, the Messiah of Nazareth. Peter took him by the hand to help him up.' He had a sense of strength coursing through his feet and ankles and he found they could take his weight. First, he stood. Then he jumped and started walking and jumping alternately. He found his voice and began audibly to praise God ecstatically, holding on to Peter and John as his greatest ever benefactors. A crowd ran to where he was, recognizing him as the crippled beggar who always sat at that gate and were astonished beyond words at what had happened.

A Pattern

This seems not to have been just an incident. It looks as if we might have a pattern. Jesus found blind beggars in the temple and at Jericho and instead of giving them money gave them their sight or their ability to walk. Peter and John faced with a beggar lame from birth,

do not give him money but cause him to walk
and to jump. Later in a heathen situation in
Lystra, he sees a lame man and detects that he
has faith to be healed and tells him in a loud
voice. 'Stand up straight on your feet!' He too
jumped up and started walking around. And
there is no record of any giving to beggars.
Three out of four of these healings led to
controversy. We will look at the controversy
after this lame man was healed in succeeding
chapters.

Here, however, we need to note that the
persons were given the means of earning a
living and relieved of the need to beg. They
were taken out of a life of dependency on
others and given the opportunity to work and
look after themselves and others. This is as big
a jump as any physical leap that this man made,
especially when he had such a lucrative pitch
at the gate of the Temple. He was enabled to
leave the category of the financially impotent
and to enter the church as a whole person.

Am I reading too much into this story?
Perhaps, but today in many countries we have
a lot of experience of throwing money at
problems that leave the situation unchanged
and sometimes worse. At least the followers
of Jesus, even if they do not have a gift of
healing, always need to ask if there is not

something better we can do for the homeless, the disabled and those in a poverty trap than salve our conscience by giving money.

Relief or Empowerment

This has implications for how we behave. In the 1960s in Nairobi, Kenya we had a lot of beggars on the streets. People in the church wondered what they ought to do when confronted by them. We learned of a piece of research done by the local branch of The Round Table. They had someone watch a beggar for a week at an average site to see how much he received from his begging. They registered every time something went into his tin and reckoned it to be a coin of the smallest denomination in the currency. They found that he was taking four times the average wage of a labourer or domestic servant at that time. It made us think again.

We had noticed the story of Blind Bartimaeus and the absence of Jesus ever giving alms and decided to set up a group and a fund into which we put five percent of the church offerings and left it open for others to contribute as they were moved to do so. Out of that we supported those working with the poor in ways to help them help themselves and also established a personal link with these places. Among them were Joytown for Crippled Children and the Thika School for the Blind, both run by the Salvation Army. This continued for years and provided a better way of helping needy people without locking them in to the cycle of begging. It gave the lame and the blind the chance to ask for something different from money.

Dependency is a choice. Sometimes it may look inevitable, but it is never entirely inevitable, in the person's heart, at least. The lame man asked for one thing, but received something much better and it was an apostle that showed him the option.

5

Peter

Why he was not Surprised

Acts 3:11-26

An Opportunity

Peter and John were in the temple again in an afternoon. Crowds of people were running towards them to see a man jumping up and down, who would not let go his hold on them. He had just been healed of his lameness and for the first time in his more than forty years he could stand on his own two feet and walk and jump around. He was ecstatic and kept loudly praising God. The crowd was growing by the minute and amazement spread from face to face when they saw the man whom they knew as the lame beggar at the gate 'Beautiful', fully mobile and full of praise.

Peter saw the questions that were written all over their faces and spontaneously seized the opportunity to answer them. He began with a question of his own. 'Why are you surprised at this and why do you stare at us?' It shows how used he was becoming to the power of God working in their new community of believers, when he could chide them for their astonishment. He proceeds to tell them why he was not surprised.

A Disclaimer

The first thing he did, however, was to deny categorically that this healing was in any sense something that he or John had done. They had no special powers; nor was it that they were so holy that God used them in this way. It was God who had done it. This was a big change from the bombastic Peter that we meet in the gospels. It is notable also that neither he or any of the apostles in the Acts were men striving after greatness or kudos for themselves. Quite the opposite! They saw themselves as mere instruments in the hand of God, even calling themselves his 'slaves' (Acts 4:29). St Vincent de Paul once said, 'The reason why God is so great a lover of humility is because he is so great a lover of truth. Humility is nothing but the truth while pride is nothing but lying.' Peter and the Apostles were content with the truth.

A Charge

Peter identified himself with the crowd by calling them 'Fellow Israelites' (Acts 3:12). They were all descendants of Abraham, Isaac and Jacob and that was a great privilege. But they were failing to recognize that their great God had given divine glory to his Servant Jesus in the miracles and wonders he had performed through him. Worse than that, they had handed Jesus over to the authorities and rejected him in the presence of Pontius Pilate, even after Pilate had decided to set him free. Still more shamefully, although they knew him to be holy and good, they rejected him and instead asked Pilate to do them the favour of turning loose a murderer called Barabbas. In effect, he charged, it was they who had killed the one who was the Prince of Life (Acts 3:13).

This was not the first or the last time Peter levied this charge against the people or their leaders (Acts 4:10, 5:30). Peter was unequivocal in laying the responsibility for the crucifixion of Jesus at their door.

A Deeper Level

Peter levied this charge without anger. We begin to notice this in the language he uses, when he calls Jesus, God's 'Servant'. This must have come from another of these sessions in the forty days between the resurrection and the ascension where Jesus was pointing out the passages in the OT scriptures that referred to himself (Luke 24:27, 45, Acts 1:2,3). It was from Isaiah 52-53 and the Servant in these chapters was not at that time recognized by the Jews as referring to the coming Messiah. They had no thought about him being wounded for our transgression or bruised for our iniquities. There was no expectation in Jesus day of a suffering Messiah. Only a conquering Messiah. Jesus, however, in his life and after his resurrection insisted that these passages about the suffering servant referred to him.

In his speech to the witnesses of the healing of the lame man, Peter uses this title, 'Servant' of Jesus to soften their culpability for his death. 'I know that what you and your leader did to Jesus was due to your ignorance. God had announced long ago through all the prophets that his Messiah **had to suffer** and he made it come true in this way' – through you. (Acts 3:18) He was not excusing them. They were still responsible for what they had done but there were things happening at a deeper level that transformed this judicial murder into a sacrifice for the sins of the world, even including theirs.

On the strength of this revelation that they had received from Jesus and God's dramatic endorsement of it in raising him after he was crucified, Peter twice called his fellow countrymen to repent and turn to God and have their sins wiped way (Acts 3:19,26). He made this sound a very attractive proposition. He used a word that they knew meant to totally sponge away the writing on a sheet of papyrus. They could start again with a clean sheet. Peter himself knew how sensational it was to have his own part in the crucifixion wiped clean from his conscience and his memory, as he comes to them gently with the same fantastic offer.

An Interim

This was not all he had to say. He made it clear that if they repented and turned to God, everything would not automatically be wonderful thereafter. Yes, there would be times, regular times of spiritual refreshment that would come to them from the Lord. But for the present, Jesus, their Messiah, had to remain in heaven until the time came for all things to be made new. This bit they knew about. All the prophets had described a golden age that would be ushered in when Messiah came. Peter explained that this was still very much in the future, but none the less sure for that (Acts3:20-21,24-25). This time he goes back to their father Abraham and God's promise to him that all the people on earth would be blessed, not just the Jews. It was going to take time to get the blessing to the whole world. They were only the first instalment.

A New Moses

Peter has one more OT jewel for them, to let them know how to behave in the interim period. Jesus was not only the suffering Servant, he was the new Moses. 'For Moses said, "The Lord your God will send you a prophet, just as he sent me, and he will be one of your own people. You are to obey everything that he tells you to do. Anyone who does not obey that prophet shall be separated from God's people and destroyed"' (Acts 3:22-23). Jesus, the new Moses would teach them what to do and how to behave in the meantime. There would be judgment if they failed to heed him.

There were overtones here that they would know warned them against going to any other sources for knowledge or instruction. In the original words of Moses, he warned them, 'Don't let your people practise divination or look for omens or use spells or charms, and don't let them consult the spirits of the dead. The LORD your God hates people who do these disgusting things, and that is why he is driving those nations out of the land as you advance. Be completely faithful to the LORD.' (Dt.18:10-13) It will not be long until these alternative claims of revelation will be confronting them.

The NOW and the NOT YET

Peter knew there was trouble ahead for him and for them all (John 21:18-19). He had made the mistake once already in being too starry eyed and optimistic (Matt.16:21-23). He had been given a living hope by the resurrection of Jesus from the dead. There was however a long furrow to plough before he and all of them received the wonderful inheritance that awaited them. They needed from the beginning to realize that some things were to be in the NOW category. Other things would be deferred to the NOT YET. A great deal of the trouble we experience as Christians comes from insisting on something hastening NOW when it is in the NOT YET. Equally we are in trouble if we drag our feet and put into the NOT YET what we can very well do and realize NOW. There would be recurring times of refreshing NOW. There was enough instruction for them to be getting on with

NOW and they would have the power to obey these instructions. Some things, however, are reserved in heaven for us while we are kept by the power of God in the present.

Joni Eareckson Tada had a diving accident that left her as a quadriplegic crippled person. She tells her own story. 'Shortly after I was injured, I read wonderful promises from Scripture like 1 John 5:14, 'This is the confidence we have in approaching God; that if we ask anything according to his will, he hears us. I prayed in faith that God would hear me and heal me, but my fingers and toes still did not move. I went back to 1 John 5:14 and read it closer. That's when it struck me. It did not say if we ask we will receive anything we think we might like or anything that would make life easier, but we will receive anything that's actually according to his will.

But friends said to me, "Why in the world would it be God's will to deny a Christian's request for healing?" That's a good question, but for every verse seeming to guarantee positive answers to our prayers for an easier happier, more healthy life, there are countless verses about the good things suffering can bring.' Joni had to learn that healing for her was not a NOW, but a NOT YET and how many people she has helped by that attitude!

More growth

All this material from Peter's mouth arose from the people's amazement at the healing of the cripple at the temple gate. Peter's second great speech built on his first. He seized the opportunity and showed how much he took seriously Jesus' original prophecy that he and the others would catch people instead of fish. He was eminently successful and drew in a large catch that day. 'But many who heard the message believed; and the number of men grew to about 5,000' (Acts 4:4). If we compare this with the 3,000 after his first speech, this means that the community multiplied by more than three times in this short period. In addition, they enjoyed the goodwill of all the people (Acts 2:47). It was looking very good for the new gospel.

6

The Sadducees

Corruption and Resurrection

Acts 4:1-22, 5:17-21

In the middle of the sunny euphoria that surrounded the healing of the lame beggar, a cloud overshadowed the crowd of people in Solomon's Porch in the temple. 'Some priests, the officer in charge of the temple guards, and some Sadducees arrived. They were annoyed...' not because a man had been healed. They could have passed over that welcome event. No, they were annoyed, 'because the two apostles were teaching the people that Jesus had risen from death, which proved that the dead will rise to life' (Acts 4:2).

An Establishment Intervention

The significant word to note is the 'Sadducees'. They were a party who had existed for a long time but came into prominence about a century before our story. They were mostly priests and had infiltrated the families of the chief priests who controlled the levers of power under the Romans. Their arrival in the temple was an intervention by the Jewish establishment of the day. The officer in charge of the temple guards was with them. He was the nearest thing to a chief police officer that they had. He was second only to the High Priest in political ranking. His presence spelled trouble.

The intervention had nothing to do with public order or any law that had been broken. It was specifically because of Peter's claim that God had raised Jesus from death. The Sadducees did not believe in the resurrection of the dead (Acts 23:8). Theirs was a materialistic kind of religion. Their opposition to the idea of resurrection was so strong that they felt they had to nip these new ideas of Peter in the bud.

Control Freaks

Today we would call the Sadducees 'control freaks'. Their primary drive was to stay in power and enjoy the benefits of their position. Their overriding method was to dominate those around them and remove anyone who got in the way. They saw Peter and John in that category.

An Emotional Intervention

Luke says, 'They were annoyed...' The same word is translated in Acts 16:18, 'Paul became *so upset* ...' by the harassment of the fortune telling girl. It was a emotional reaction that triggered their intervention. The story that follows is peppered with negative emotional language. They are successively annoyed, puzzled, intimidated, frustrated, jealous, perplexed, afraid, furious, murderous and sadistic. (See Acts 4:2, 13,15,17,24,5:17,24,26,33,40) This is characteristic of the Sadducees. Josephus, the Jewish historian says, 'The behaviour of the Sadducees one towards another is in some degree wild; and their conversation with those that are of their own party is as barbarous as if they were strangers to them' (Wars II.8.14). On this day, they were highly emotional while dealing with a theological and legal question. Argument is never very successful when emotions are running high. It was too late in the day to investigate the matter, 'so they arrested them and put them in jail until the next day.'

A Financial Intervention

'The next day the Jewish leaders, the elders, and the teachers of the Law gathered in Jerusalem. They met with the High Priest Annas and with Caiaphas, John, Alexander, and the others who belonged to the High Priest's family.' We have met this priestly family before (See *Characters around the Cross* p.55-58). They controlled the Bazaars of Annas where Jesus upset the tables of the money changers. They were politically incestuous, cornering the tenure of the office of the High priest to father, sons and sons-in-law for more than a generation.

This family operated what we would call a Mafia today. Josephus says, 'As for Annas, the high priest, he increased in glory every day and this to a great degree, and had obtained the favour and the esteem of the citizens in a signal manner; for he was a great hoarder up of money. He therefore cultivated the friendship of Albinus (The Roman Governor) and of the current high priest, by making them presents; he also had servants who were very wicked, who joined themselves to the boldest sort of the people and went to the threshing floors and took away the tithes that belonged to the priests by violence, and did not refrain from beating such as would not give these tithes to them. So the other high priests acted in like manner as did those his servants, without anyone being able to prohibit them; so that some of the priests that of old were wont to be supported by these tithes died for want of food. (Ant.20.9.2) The Sadducees were greedy.

Accountability Denied

Although they were priests, they were quite irresponsible and it was their beliefs that allowed them to be so. Josephus again, 'The Sadducees are those who take away fate entirely and suppose that God is not concerned in our doing or not doing what is evil. And they say that to act what is good or what is evil is at men's own choice, and that the one or the other belongs to every one so that they may act as they please. They also take away the belief of the immortal duration of the soul and the punishments and rewards of Hades.' (Ant.13.5.9)

The Sadducees view of God gave them unlimited autonomy of behaviour. Their belief that there was no resurrection and no after life removed any restraint on their surly behaviour. Today also, our secular society has edited God and heaven and hell out of our consciousness. This can be seen in the sophistication of the existentialist writer Jean Paul Sartre when he maintained, 'Rationally, the universe is absurd and you must try to authenticate yourself. How? By an act of the will. So, if you are driving along down a street and see someone walking in the pouring rain, you stop your car, pick him up and give him a lift. It is absurd. What does it matter? He is nothing. The situation is nothing, but you have authenticated yourself by an act of the will. But the difficulty is that the authentification has no rational or logical content. All directions of an act of the will are equal. Therefore, if you are driving along and see the man in the rain, speed up and knock him down, you have in equal measure authenticated your will.'

It can be seen equally in everyday life, when an elderly woman in Yorkshire is fatally mugged for fish and chips she had just gone out to buy for her supper. If there is no God to care or judge, there is no need to be nice or considerate or kind. You can be rude or violent with anyone and it makes no difference. That is how the Sadducees thought. That is how people are thinking today. They provide us with a perfect illustration of what our beliefs are doing to our society. Financial fraud, protection rackets, price cartels, shop lifting, muggings, burglaries, petty theft, bold faced lying are increasingly a curse in our societies. We try to tackle them with new laws and regulations. These measures need to be undertaken but they will not be successful so long as the underlying beliefs are left untouched.

So, when Peter said that God raised Jesus from death, it was serious for the Sadducees. It was not just a matter of philosophical belief. It meant they were accountable in this life and the next for all the fraud, intimidation and violence they had perpetrated. The prosperity of an obscenely rich family was at stake. Jesus risen from the dead, has the same implications for our behaviour today. It means we will have to give an account to God.

Hiding behind Bureaucracy

The next day the High Priest convened a meeting of the Sanhedrin or Great Council of the Jews. They did not want to act on their own. They were not popular with the people. Like many political heavyweights, they meant to hide behind the façade of officialdom. They sat in their places in the august semi-circular Hall of Hewn Stone and stood the two apostles in front of them. They posed a leading question about the healing, 'How did you do this? What power have you got or whose name did you use?' (Acts 4:7)

Peter gave a forthright answer, 'This man stands here before you completely well through the power of the name of Jesus Christ of Nazareth – whom you crucified and whom God raised from death.' He then quoted a saying that originated from the building of the original temple by Solomon. All the masonry was prefabricated off site and only assembled on Temple mount. Legend had it that they kept coming on a stone that would not fit anywhere and they just pushed it aside until it was buried out of sight. Then, when they were short of a stone for the head of the corner, they found that the awkwardly shaped stone fitted perfectly. 'The stone that you the builders despised turned out to be the most important of all.' He was saying that they rejected Jesus but now God had raised him from death and shown how absolutely unique he was. 'Salvation is to be found through him alone; in all the world there is no one else whom God has given who can save us.'

Amazed and Dumbfounded

Peter caught them off balance. He was not in the slightest intimidated by either the setting of the Hall of Hewn Stone or the full council in all their regalia. He was fearlessly outspoken with a competence that did not match their view of them as uneducated laymen from the North. They attributed this to the influence of Jesus on them and they were at a loss as to what to do next. The resurrection was producing people who could not contrast more with the kind of people the Sadducees were. Peter and John, by their boldness, took away any tame excuses they might have made for their unscrupulous behaviour.

Their own question about the lame beggar's healing had backfired on them for the simple reason that he was standing there in front of them with two prisoners whom they could not intimidate. So, like good bureaucrats they called for a closed session to give them time to privately discuss the matter and decide what to do. They did not get any further in private. Their impotence to do anything was, if anything, increased.

Threats to no Purpose
They resorted to threats intended to terrorize Peter and John into being silent and give up speaking and teaching in the name of Jesus. Without hesitation, the two apostles shifted the ground of the discussion and put their judges on the defensive. Their answer was, 'You yourselves judge which is right in God's sight – to obey you or to obey God. For we cannot stop speaking of what we ourselves have seen and heard.' The Sadducees were not ready for this challenge to their authority in the name of God. All they could do was issue them with even more threats and release them. They saw

that it was impossible to punish them, because the people were all praising God for what had happened.

There followed a short interval, probably of weeks, during which the apostles continued to preach and heal people. The new community grew in size and favour with the people, not just in the city, but from the towns around Jerusalem in the province of Judea (Acts 5:12-16).

God in Control

The increasing popularity and success of the apostles made the High Priest and all his Sadducee companions extremely jealous. They decided to take tougher measures, so they arrested all the apostles and put them in the public jail pending trial the next day. But that night an angel of the Lord opened the prison gates, led the apostles out, and said to them, 'Go and stand in the Temple, and tell the people all about this new life.' The apostles obeyed, and at dawn they entered the Temple and started teaching.

Without knowing about any of this, 'The High Priest and his companions called together all the Jewish elders for a full meeting of the Council; then they sent orders to the prison to have the apostles brought before them. But when the officials arrived, they did not find the apostles in prison, so they returned to the Council and reported, 'When we arrived at the jail, we found it locked up tight and all the guards on watch at the gates; but when we opened the gates, we found no one inside!'

What an embarrassment! When the chief priests and the officer in charge of the temple guards heard this, they were totally perplexed about what had happened to the apostles. Then a man came in and said to them, 'Listen! The men you put in prison are in the Temple teaching the people!' So the officer went off with his men and brought the apostles back. They did not use force, however, because they were afraid that the people might lynch them. (Acts 5:17-26)

This is always the end of those who set their hearts on controlling people and things. In one way or another, God confounds them and brings them down. It may take a long time, but God does not give his glory to another.

Eliminate the Opposition?

They brought the apostles in, made them stand before the Council, and the High Priest, panic stricken, questioned them. 'We gave you strict orders not to teach in the name of this man,' he said; 'but see what you have done! You have spread your teaching all over Jerusalem, and you want to make us responsible for his death!' Their fear was escalating.

When they expressed this growing fear, they showed that they had not been listening to any of the preaching, so Peter spells it out again. He and the other apostles went back to the issue of obedience where they had left off (Acts 4:19), 'We must **obey** God, not men. The God of our ancestors raised Jesus from death, after you had killed him by nailing him to a cross. God raised him to his right-hand side as Leader and Saviour, to give the people of Israel the opportunity to repent and have their sins forgiven. We are witnesses to these things – we and the Holy Spirit, who is God's gift to those who **obey** him.'

Yes, they had been laying responsibility for Jesus' death at their door, but not in a vindictive way to get them persecuted or put out of office. They wanted them to repent and have their sins forgiven. The political question to the apostles was whether to obey constituted authority when to do so was to disobey what God was telling them to do. The Sadducees seemed completely deaf to those strains of the apostles' speech. They could only react emotionally. They were furious. They were murderous. They were ready to have the apostles all put to death. They were desperate. Like all control freaks, they were ready to get rid of those who seemed to stand in their way.

They were out of their mind to even think such thoughts. To begin with they had no power to impose the death penalty. For that they had to get the Romans to sanction that. Then the popularity of the apostles was so high, that they looked ready to stone the soldiers whom they sent to arrest them in the temple.

A Temporary Respite

Fortunately, they were not all Sadducees in the Council. There were some Pharisees also who believed in the resurrection and one of them, Gamaliel, suggested that they let this take its course for a while longer to see if it would not just fizzle out as other such scares had done. This cooled them down and they followed Gamaliel's advice. From wanting to execute them, they backed down to only having them flogged and dismissed with further threats if they continued to preach about Jesus.

Modern Sadducees

Our admiration for Peter and the apostles is boundless, but it has not always stayed like that in the churches. We have sometimes become more like Judaism that opposed them. Now we have Sadducean Bishops, Moderators, Clergy, Elders and Deacons, control freaks in the churches. For them, even in office the key words are control, covetousness, and personal autonomy, the Sadducean trio of values. But before we crow too much, we have Sadducees in our offices, factories, businesses also. They use downsizing and reorganization to reinforce their control and bribery to get business or to coax compliance from colleagues.

Our homes are not exempt from this curse. Sadducean parents and spouses can make life a misery for the rest of the family. So Peter and the Sadducees present us with two very different role models. Which will we follow?

7

Peter

The Solid Rock

Acts 4:1-22, 5:17-42

The first test of the Jerusalem church was when the might of the Jewish state ranged itself against them. They were fast moving towards the critical mass in numbers for the survival of a new movement (Acts 4:3). The experience of Jesus showed that early popularity could fall off very rapidly when less palatable truths offended people (John 6:66). His parable of the sower showed his own awareness of the effect that persecution could have (Mark 4:16-17). The new church was very fragile. It would be a miracle if it survived. It is hard to exaggerate how much the future of Christianity hinged on Peter and John at this juncture.

The trigger for the onslaught was the speech Peter made when explaining the healing of the lame man to the people in the temple. He repeated what he had said in the Pentecost

speech. 'God raised Jesus from death' (Acts
2:24,32, 3:15) and demonstrated that he was
the long awaited Messiah whom the people of
Israel should accept as their leader. (Acts 2:36,
3:18,20) This was enough for the authorities
to feel they had to act, so they had Peter and
John arrested and put in jail. The next day they
convened the ruling council, arraigned the two
apostles before it and interrogated them about
how the man had been healed.

A Consistent Message

Peter did not change his story. What he had
told the people, (chapter 5) he now told their
leaders. The power to heal the cripple was the
same power as God used when he raised Jesus
from death and demonstrated that he was the
Messiah (Acts 4:10-11). He repeated the same
message in the much more tense atmosphere
of their second trial, (Acts 5:30-31) and after
they were released (Acts 5:42).

Peter had been the first to realize and say
that Jesus was the Messiah while Jesus was still
alive (Matt 16:16). As soon as Peter said this,
Jesus warned them all of the opposition he first,
and they later, would face. Peter objected with
some vigour, but was severely rebuked for his
presumption (Matt.16:21-27). He lived to see
that Jesus was right about himself. He was

crucified, but, as he predicted, he rose on the third day. Now Peter was finding out that Jesus was right about the opposition they would face. But he did not back down in the slightest. Jesus was the Messiah and the proof was that God had raised him from death. He was rock solid in his consistency.

A Unique Saviour

He went a step further. With the help of a quotation from a Psalm (118:22) he affirmed that Jesus was the only Saviour. 'Jesus is the one of whom the scripture says: "The stone that you the builders despised turned out to be the most important of all." Salvation is to be found through him alone; in all the world there is no one else whom God has given who can save us.' (Acts 4:11-12) (See p.76)

Saving was the business Jesus was in (Luke19:9). It was clearly also the business that Peter and the apostles were in. In his Pentecost speech, Peter announced that those who called on the name of the Lord would be **saved.** He urged his hearers to **save** themselves from this wicked generation. Luke records that the Lord added to their group those who were being saved (Acts 2:21,40,47). The authorities who were trying them were wanting to know how the cripple had been **saved (**healed). God had raised Jesus to his right hand side a Leader and a **Saviour** (Acts 5:31).

'Saved' is a word that means different things to different people. The things from which Jesus is the only Saviour were sin, the present wicked generation and the wrath to come (Luke3:7). Peter regarded this salvation as absolutely necessary ('We must be saved' Acts 4:12) and Jesus as the only one who could effect it. He was still saying this at the end of his life (1 Pet 4:18).

This language is less used today. Indeed it is sometimes mocked. If one answers yes to the question, 'Are you saved?' it might well evoke the response, 'Well, not from impertinence!'

An Undisputed Lord

When the council forbade Peter and John to speak or teach in the name of Jesus, they demurred because they felt they had a higher loyalty. On this occasion they introduced the possibility that there might be a conflict between obeying the Council and obeying God, by posing a question. 'You yourselves judge which is right in God's sight to obey you or to obey God' (Acts 4:19). They implied that they knew the answer and it was likely to persuade them not to heed what the Council was asking them to do. At the second trial, and after a lot more preaching, they were more emphatic. 'We must obey God and not men!' (Acts 5:29). Perhaps this was because during the previous night, Peter had actually been told by an angel who opened the prison gate, where they were being held, for them, 'Go, stand in the temple and tell the people about this new life!' (Acts 5:20) Whatever the reason, they were even more insistent than before that they had a higher loyalty than that to the Council.

Peter had said in the Pentecost speech, 'God has made this Jesus whom you crucified both LORD and Messiah' (Acts 2:36). The word for LORD was KURIOS. It was used both for the Roman Emperor and for God. It puts this discussion between Peter and the Council in the same frame as the word of Jesus. 'Render to Caesar the things that are Caesar's and to God the things that are God's!' (Mark 12:17) Peter was bound to obey God, even if it conflicted with a human authority, that he would in normal circumstances accept.

Jesus had warned them that they would be hauled before both political and religious authorities for the sake of the gospel, but not to worry because the Holy Spirit would teach them at the time what to say (Luke 12:12, 21:12-15). This word about obeying God and not men is clearly what Peter was taught to say at this time and it is consistent with the whole tenor of the New Testament. The gospel must not be either muffled or modified by human authorities, religious or political. Where it has been subject to the civil power, it has always been compromised.

This necessity of obeying the Lord and not men motivated Martin Luther when tried in the presence of the Emperor Charles in 1521. Pressed to repudiate the books he had written and the errors they contained, he replied, 'Since Your Majesty and your lordships desire a simple reply I will answer without horn and without teeth. Unless I am convinced by Scripture and plain reason – I do not accept the authority of popes and councils, for they have contradicted each other – my conscience is captive to the Word of God. I cannot and I will not recant anything for to go against conscience is neither right or safe. Here I stand. I can do no other. God help me! Amen.'

An Overruling God

As soon as Peter and John were set free, they returned to their group and told them what the chief priests and the elders had said. When the believers heard it, they all joined together in prayer to God. It was remarkable praying. It was full of the sense that God was in control.

Just as he had been at work when Jesus himself had been tried and condemned and crucified, so he was in control of what was happening to them. Their concern was not to be spared further persecution. They laid the threats that had been made to them before God. 'And now, Lord, take notice of the threats they have made, and allow us, your servants, to speak your message with all boldness. Stretch out your hand to heal, and grant that wonders and miracles may be performed through the name of your holy Servant Jesus' (Acts 4:29-36).

An Empowering Spirit

What was the secret of Peter's rock solid stance before the courts. It was not the stubbornness of his will. We saw how weak he was in the courtyard of the High Priest's house when he denied any knowledge of Jesus. Luke makes it clear that his secret was that he was 'full of the Holy Spirit' (Acts 4:8). After their confident praying with the group to whom they reported what had happened, 'the place where they were meeting was shaken. They were all filled with the Holy Spirit and began to proclaim God's message with boldness.' When responding to the second interrogation he explained, 'We are witnesses to these things – we and the Holy Spirit, who is God's gift to those who obey him.' There was no question that this had anything to do with the temperament or character of Peter and the others. The secret of their boldness and their defiance of the Council was the fact that they were inspired inwardly, separately and together by the Holy Spirit who kept on being poured out upon them.

Someone to Die For

They did not get off with intimidating threats this time. The authorities had them flogged, which could be an excruciating and even a life threatening experience. This did not daunt them. 'They were happy, because God had considered them worthy to suffer disgrace for the sake of Jesus'(Acts 5:40,41). Luke draws attention to their indifference to the pain they had suffered and emphasizes their joy at being identified with Jesus to the point of sharing his shame. They had found someone they would die for. It took that to make them an indestructible force in their world. This is the advantage that terrorists have over those who try to combat them. They have something they will willingly die for. There are still many Christians with that kind of faith, 164 million martyrs, on average, die each year according to the 2002 World Christian Handbook table.

There seem not to be so many in the West and until we share the kind of faith to die for that sustained Peter and the earliest Christians, we should not be surprised if we continue to decline.

Jesus had placed great hopes on Peter. He had given him a name to live up to (John 1:42). He had said he would be foundational to the church (Matt.16:18). Even with foreknowledge of Peter's denial, he had still seen him as the one who would put backbone into the rest (Luke22:32). After the resurrection, he commissioned Peter to feed and tend his sheep and lambs (John 21:15-17). We have seen him rise to these challenges and nowhere more than when he faced the Council and came close to losing his life.

Archbishop Cranmer (1489-1556) came to this loyalty late. He had stood for the real faith, but in the face of Queen Mary's persecution he signed six recantations by which he hoped to purchase his life. No sooner had he signed them than he was wretched. In the end he recanted his recantations and went to be burned at the stake in Oxford.

As he spoke to the people before he was burned, he said, 'Now I come to the great thing that troubles my conscience more than any other thing that ever I said or did in my life.

That is setting abroad writings contrary to the truth. Here I now renounce and refute these things written by my hand contrary to the truth which I thought in my heart and wrote for fear of death to save my life. And forasmuch as my hand offended in writing contrary to my heart, my hand therefore shall be the first punished. For, if I come to the fire, it shall be the first burnt.' And as he came to the stake, he said, 'This was the hand that wrote it, therefore it shall first suffer punishment.' And holding it steadily in the flame, he never stirred nor cried till life was gone.

Neither Peter nor Cranmer were perfect, yet their loyalty reasserted itself and both contributed to faith in Jesus in ways that still are felt today.

8

Gamaliel

Hedging your Bets

Acts 5:33-39

Just when the apostles were about to be lynched by the Jewish authorities, help came from an unexpected source. From within the Council a man stood up and put another view before them. His name was Gamaliel.

An Unusual Pharisee

Gamaliel was a Pharisee, the same party as continually harassed Jesus during his life on earth. We have a caricature of them as being censorious, judgmental, hypocritical, self deceived and self-righteous. Certainly, Jesus had lots of negative and uncomplimentary things to say about them (Matt.23). In point of fact, though they were bad, they were not seen to be as bad as the Sadducees. If we accept the descriptions of Josephus the Jewish historian, he contrasts them like this, summarized by A.J. Saldarin in *Pharisees, Scribes and Sadducees.*

Pharisees: Affectionate with each other and cultivate harmonious relations with the community.
Sadducees: Boorish with each other. As rude to their peers as to aliens.

Pharisees: Attribute everything to fate or to God.
Sadducees: They deny fate. God is beyond both the committing and the very spirit of evil.

Pharisees: To act rightly or wrongly rests mostly with humans but fate co-operates in each action.
Sadducees: Humans are totally in control of the choice of good or evil.

Pharisees: Every soul is imperishable.
Sadducees: There is no endurance of the soul.

Pharisees: Only the souls of the good pass into another kind of body. The souls of the wicked suffer eternal punishment.
Sadducees: There are no rewards or punishments.

Pharisees: They were considered the most accurate interpreters of the law.

Sadducees: They accepted only the law of Moses and not the traditions.

Gamaliel was even more congenial than the general run of the Pharisees. He was the grandson of the great Hillel, the founder of the most influential school of the Pharisees. He rose to great distinction within the party himself. He became the first of only seven men in history accorded the title of Rabban or Master Rabbi. He taught Saul of Tarsus (Acts 22:3). The stories told about him show that he was not infected by the narrow bigotry of the sect. He did not object to Greek learning. He rose above the prejudices of his party. Candour and wisdom seem to have been the features of his character. This fits with Luke's comment that 'he was highly respected by all the people' (Acts 5:34). He was a member of the Seventy person Council of the Jews as were many Pharisees. On this day he was in the middle of the emotion that was being hyped up in the trial of the twelve apostles. He decided to intervene and try to calm things down. He stood up to speak and asked for those on trial to be sent out, while they heard and discussed what he had to say.

A Timely Intervention

He began by advising caution and took an historic approach in his argument. He was really playing for time. There were frequent uprisings and seditious movements against the Roman occupying power in Judea at that time. Gamaliel referred to two of them who had blustered up, attracted followers, ran their course and fizzled out. 'You remember that Theudas appeared some time ago, claiming to be somebody great, and about four hundred men joined him. But he was killed, all his followers were scattered, and his movement died out. After that, Judas the Galilean appeared during the time of the census; he drew a crowd after him, but he also was killed, and all his followers were scattered. And so in this case, I tell you, do not take any action against these men' (Acts 5:36-37).

He suggested that the Council note these historic precedents and take no action. It is worth noting that there was considerable sloppiness in his selection of parallels. Theudas and Judas were clearly political, subversive and violent and not remotely like this pacifist, preaching forgiveness to the crowd they had before them.

A Cunning Religious Twist to the Argument

This was, in large part, a religious court packed with religious people of varying degrees of sincerity. They all paid at least lip service to God. Gamaliel played to this gallery and elevated his argument to acknowledge the Almighty. 'Leave them alone!' he said. 'If what they have planned and done is of human origin, it will disappear, but if it comes from God, you cannot possibly defeat them. You could find yourselves fighting against God!' This certainly would speak to the fatalism of the Pharisees and even the Sadducees would have a hard time arguing for human initiative after it had been so crisply and openly stated. It had the added advantage that it was a sentiment that Jesus had himself expressed. 'Every plant which my Father in heaven did not plant will be pulled up' (Matt. 15:13).

It was an incredibly subtle injection into the debate. Most present including Gamaliel would accept it because they wanted to believe that the Jesus movement would fizzle out as had the political uprisings of Theudas and Judas. In fact, Gamaliel was implying this by using these examples. By going along with their bias, however, Gamaliel was smoothing feathers, by making them believe they would never willingly be found fighting against God. He won the day. The apostles were not executed. Another crisis had been successfully passed.

Possible Motivations

It is interesting to ask what motivated Gamaliel to intervene in the Council. We know that the issue of the resurrection was foremost in the minds of the Sadducees when they swung into action against Peter and John (Acts 4:2). Pharisees did believe in the resurrection (Acts 23:6-9) and it was a point of violent dispute between these two parties. Gamaliel could have been showing himself a little supportive of the believers who were advocating the resurrection. This is hardly likely, however in view of the fact that a prayer of Gamaliel against heretics has come down to us, 'Let there be no hope to them who apostatize from the true religion; and let heretics, howsoever many they may be, all perish as in a moment; and let the kingdom of pride be speedily rooted out and broken in our days. Blessed art thou, O Lord our God, who destroyest the wicked and bringest down the proud,' (*Life and Epistles of Paul* by Conyers and Howson. P.48)

The more likely factor that motivated Gamaliel to say his piece was fear of the reaction

of the Roman authorities. If they took the law
into their own hands and imposed the death
penalty on this now prominent group of
leaders where there was no political
infringement, it would not stand well with
them. Gamaliel would remember what a
palaver they had to inveigle Pontius Pilate into
giving the order for Jesus to be crucified. Reprisals
on the Council from the Roman governor
would hurt all the parties that made it up.
Gamaliel would have wanted to prevent that.

His motive may have been more simply just
to diffuse a tense situation. There are people with
temperaments that find it very difficult to bear
conflict. To avoid it they, almost
unconsciously learn peace making skills. I
recall this happening in a denominational
Assembly some years ago. In the middle of a
very intense debate, when no one could see a
way out of the impasse, a Minister stood up.
He recommended that we send it back to the
churches and went on, 'If they say let us not
do this, Well!…If they say do it, Well! Well!'
and the session collapsed in laughter. The
tension was eased. 'In the Myers Briggs Type
Indicator (MBTI) people like this are INFP's
or 'Mediators'. They can be a gift to a team if
they function positively. They can foster
indecision if they function in an unhealthy way.

Doubtful Outcomes

We are now able, from our standpoint, to assess Gamaliel's action in its historical perspective, just as he tried to do with Theudas and Judas. Was the outcome good for the Church? It certainly gave them respite even if it was only temporary. It also preserved the apostles for future work. This was no mean result when we consider how much of the New Testament we owe to Peter and John.

Was it a good result for the Sanhedrin? All it did was postpone the day when they would go over the top and have Stephen stoned to death (Acts7:54-58). It did little to mitigate the social and political turmoil of the times which eventually called down on them the wrath of the Roman Empire, the destruction of their city in AD70 and the end of their nation in AD131.

We have to be grateful to Gamaliel. His firm grip on the truth that God works all things after the good counsel of his will is to be commended (Eph.1:11). It is probably also wise when there is an argument verging on violence, to urge people to delay and think again. Finally, we cannot forget the word of Jesus, 'Blessed are the peacemakers: for they shall be called the children of God' (Matt.5:9).

9

Ananias and Sapphira

The View at the Apostles' Feet

Acts 5:1-11

The First Couple in the Church

There are so many things we would like to
know about Ananias and Sapphira. Apart from
the Apostle, Mary and Barnabas, they are the
first proper names mentioned so far in the early
church. They were the first named married
couple and there was really only one other
named couple we are sure about, Priscilla and
Aquila in the rest of the NT. (Acts18:2 etc.)
We do know some things about them. They
were married and owned some land. Was it a
plot of agricultural land back in their ancestral
home district somewhere in the countryside?
It is generally assumed that the field Barnabas
sold was back in Cyprus where he came from
(Acts4:36). Was it a small piece of real estate
in the city of Jerusalem that was valuable for
building on? We do not know.

We know that it was not a male dominated household, for they took decisions jointly about finance. Today they would have had a joint bank account. They were both generous and ready to let their faith affect fairly drastically their attitude to money.

Had they known Jesus? Were they among the 120 believers who stayed together between the resurrection and Pentecost? Were they converts at or after the Pentecost response? I tend to think they were post Pentecost. If they had known or heard Jesus, they could hardly have tried on the hypocritical ploy they got into.

The Apostles' Feet

The sale of property and possessions to supply the common purse had been going on from day one of the new community (Acts2:45). How it was done physically is not described until Barnabas brought the proceeds of his Cyprus property. 'He laid it at the apostles' feet.' It was not just Peter's feet for it is the plural 'apostles' that is used. There is not much to indicate precisely what this meant. Teachers sat to instruct their followers (Luke5:3). 'Mary sat down at the feet of the Lord and listened to his teaching' (Luke10:39). 'Paul was brought up at the feet of Gamaliel' (Acts22:3). It might have been a spot on the ground in front of where the apostles sat in front of the gathering of believers. We can assume that it was a public act, visible to all present and that the amount of what was given, was known (Acts5:8). Maybe this was the trouble.

Joseph the Levite literally got a name for himself, 'Barnabas' which means 'one who encourages'. It is mentioned in the first reference to him as the substantial donor of a significant amount of money (Acts4:33-37). Was it this that gave Ananias and Sapphira the idea that if they matched the generosity of Barnabas, it might get them honour from the apostles too?

Sociologists say that there are three things that motivate people to give. 'Social exchange' is where there is a calculation as to what the giving will do for the donor. In Europe, the Values Study in 1980 showed that this is the major motivation for voluntary giving in UK. In Kenya, to raise funds they hold a 'Harambee'. This is a public occasion where people and groups come to give. They take their donation to the platform and the goods or the amounts are read out to all present. I once read a consultants report on Fund raising in Nigeria where the experts said that it was useless to try and raise funds in Nigeria unless the amounts and the donors were given great publicity. This was the approach of the Pharisees in Jesus day whereas he advised that we should not let our right hand know what our left hand was doing (Matt.6:2-4).

'Beneficence' describes those whose sole concern is to share what they have with those who are less fortunate than themselves.

'Solidarity' is the word they use for those who want to get alongside and identify with the needy persons and work with them at improving their lot. Fewest donors are in this third category.

What happened at the apostles' feet apparently pushed Ananias and Sapphira into the 'social exchange' category. They set out to give the impression of giving more than they were actually giving. 'With his wife's agreement he kept part of the money for himself and handed the rest over to the apostles' (Acts5:2). They were obviously trying to be upsides with Barnabas and others. We wonder if 'the apostles' feet' method of receiving gifts was really a good idea. Yet in one of the churches where I was Pastor, I had an elderly deacon who liked this idea of the gifts being laid at the apostles feet. He said it was his experience that those who emphasized the bit about the right hand and the left hand, did so because they wanted to give less rather than more!

An Ominous Hark Back

Luke is always giving himself away by his careful use of words, making points that are only discernible to the discerning. He uses a word for this holding back of part of the money by Ananias and Sapphira that signals that this is not the first time this kind of thing had happened at the beginning of a new movement. The word is only used earlier in one place in the Greek OT. It is right at the very beginning of the Israelite campaign to occupy the promised land. When they attacked and took the city of Jericho, they were told to devote absolutely all the booty to God by destroying it (Jos.6:17-19). One man, Achan, decided to 'keep' some of the trophies for himself and his family. He buried them in the ground inside his tent. It is the same word as Luke uses for Ananias and Sapphira. Achan and his family also paid the price for their greed with their lives (Jos.7:1,25). A serious signal was being sent to the church.

The Gates of Hell

Peter said to him, , 'Ananias, why did you let Satan take control of you...' (Acts 5:3) One commentator prefaces his remarks on this verse by saying, 'I claim no very close or intimate familiarity with the devil.' I do not think we can say the same thing about Peter. Satan is not often referred to in the Gospels – only in eight incidents. Two of these involved Peter and they were incidents of monumental importance. The first was after Peter had said that he believed Jesus was the Messiah and then tried to rebuke Jesus for even entertaining the idea that he would suffer and die at the hands of the Jewish authorities. 'Get behind me Satan,' was Jesus' strong but ironic response. In commending Peter for his confession, he had just spoken about building his church and affirmed that the Gates of Hell would not prevail against it. Then only a sentence or two later, he is identifying Peter as the Satan who had no idea about the things of God (Matt.16:16-23).

The second incident was at the last supper. Jesus warned Peter that Satan would try again to possess him and he would succeed temporarily. It happened. Peter denied Jesus three times and it took several attempts for Jesus to get Peter back on track. So, Peter was very familiar with Satan and his methods.

We see this in the way he framed his question to Ananias. 'Why did you let Satan take control of you and make you lie (Acts5:3). The teaching of the NT is that we give Satan a foothold in our lives by instances of moral carelessness and then cannot easily extract ourselves at a critical juncture. It would seem that Judas and Ananias ceded ground to Satan by lapses into greed and then found themselves irretrievably in his power. In the case of Peter's denial it was expressions of overconfidence in himself (Luke 22:33).

All through this dialogue Peter addresses only Ananias. He uses the second person singular pronoun throughout. It is treated as a matter of personal responsibility for Ananias. Reference to Sapphira is left until she, herself, is on the scene.

In this way, the first recorded internal attack on the infant church was mounted through Ananias and Sapphira and thwarted by Peter who had learned from his own past encounters with Satan and was now controlled by the Holy Spirit.

Peter's Insight

How did Peter know that Ananias brought only part of the proceed of their sale of the land. Did he know the land they had sold? Were they from Galilee? Did Peter keep a watchful eye on the movements of the land market and know what they saw in front of them was well short of what they should have received? It is hardly likely. The only other explanation was that the Holy Spirit was so powerfully and pervasively in Peter that he 'discerned' that Ananias was acting a big lie that had to be challenged. We see Peter exercising the same insight when he confronted Simon Magus in Samaria (Acts 8:23).

Why did he make such a public display of unveiling this deception? We sense that they were in a critical situation for the survival of the 'church' first called by that name in this passage (Acts 5:11). Externally they were up against the Jewish authorities for the content of their preaching about the cross and resurrection. Here, internally, there was a threat to the other main plank of their witness, the support of the needy among them and the principles of truth and generosity that underlay both prongs of their strategy.

Who do we think we are we fooling?

What was this terrible action that Satan was intent on propelling Ananias to undertake? Peter said it was lying to the Holy Spirit. It was lying to God (Acts 5:3,4). All that Ananias thought was involved was lying to the people who witnessed their gift or who heard about it later. He with his wife's consent was prepared to risk this deception for the sake of the reputation of sacrifice and generosity it would bring them. Peter later said to Sapphira that they had decided together to put the Lord's Spirit to the test. I do not think they did this consciously. What was in their minds was most likely the good image the action of selling the land and giving the money would give them plus the things they would be able to do with the money they kept back.

In the Holy-Spirit-charged atmosphere of the church meeting, Peter called it by its real name as lying to God when they were all relying on the Holy Spirit to work his wonderful works. It was like throwing a spanner in the works. It was like causing a fuse that would shut down the whole operation. It was like damaging a longstanding friendship by being totally false to a friend.

As all this dawned powerfully on the hapless Ananias, it was too much for him and he fell down dead on the spot. It was an unexpected shock to everyone who was there and all who heard about it afterwards. According to custom, the young men wrapped the body in a shroud, carried him out and buried him (Acts 5:5-6). We are accountable to God. Everything is open to the eyes of him with whom we have to do. This was the secret of the high moral character of the early church. They lived with the sense of God's eye upon them and conscious of the kind of people he wanted them to be.

There is a story of the boy who was trying to get his friend to do something wrong. He looked to the right and then the left and said, 'Come on! There is no one here. No one will see us.' His friend said quietly, 'You forgot to look up,' And survived the temptation.

Whose is it anyway?

The sad part of this story is that it need never have happened at all. Peter told Ananias, 'Before you sold the property, it belonged to you; and after you sold it, the money was yours. Why, then, did you decide to do such a thing?' There was no compulsion to sell the land. They did not need to give the money. It was theirs to keep if they wanted to. It was a voluntary society. No one was dictating to them what to do. Sadly, everyone would have been better off if they had kept the land. But no, they wanted the approval. They wanted some things they had done without for a long time and thought up a brilliant scheme that could give them it all. It involved dishonesty and hypocrisy and that was the damning feature. Covetousness was their undoing. They coveted the reputation. They coveted a bit of extra cash and they became a very sad chapter in the history of the church.

The Chance to Back Down

About three hours later his wife, not knowing what had happened, came in all innocently. Perhaps they had agreed that she would not even say anything and give the impression of being modest and dismissive about such a generous gift. That would fit the whole tone of the event. What a surprise when Peter came right up to her. Was he going to thank her for their generosity? That is what she would have expected. Instead, he referred to the gift in a different way, with rather a rude question. 'Was it such and such an amount you received for your property?' At least he was acknowledging it, she must have thought, so 'Yes, that's right,' she replied perhaps shyly (Acts5:7-8). It was a test and she did not recognize it. It was a last chance to distance herself from her husband and be honest and say, sheepishly even, 'No, actually we got a bit more but there are some other things we want to do with the balance.' That could have saved her. But the mutual pact had been too deliberate for that and she affirmed the lie.

The Fear of the Lord.

Sadly, Peter said to her, 'Why did you and your husband decide to put the Lord's Spirit to the test? The men have just come back from burying your husband. They will carry you out too!' She too fell down at his feet and died.' The apostle's feet again! Was the gift still lying there? If it was, it would have been a telling sight to see the still form of Sapphira lying at the apostle's feet beside the tainted gift from her and her husband. 'The young men came in and saw that she was dead, so they carried her out.' (Acts 5:7-10). Alexander Whyte finishes the quote, 'and they buried Ananias and Sapphira in Aceldama next to Judas Iscariot, the proprietor of the place.' They both were destroyed by the same weakness.

'The whole church and all the others who heard of this were terrified. Many miracles and wonders were being performed among the people by the apostles. All the believers met together in Solomon's Porch. Nobody outside the group dared to join them, even though the people spoke highly of them. But more and more people were added to the group, a crowd of men and women who believed in the Lord' (Acts 5: 11-14). The fear of the Lord is the beginning of Wisdom (Proverbs 1:7).

The Church of the Saviour in Washington conducts workshops to sensitize people about the needs of the poor. One of the exercises in which they engage people is to write their own autobiography about money. They do this because they believe that we imbibe our attitudes to how we get and spend money from a very early age and it becomes almost second nature to us. If we are going to change and be generous, it means we need to be born again in this important area of our lives. It makes sense to me and when I look at the sad fate of Ananias and Sapphira, I want to do anything that would avoid the dishonesty and hypocrisy that was their undoing.

10

The Seven

Discrimination: a Threat to Growth

Acts 6:1-7

It is difficult to know what to call 'the seven' (Acts 21:8). There is a fairly consistent line taken by the early fathers, that this was the initiation of the office of 'Deacon' in the church. It is true that there did develop an office of 'Deacon' (Phil.1:1, 1 Tim.3:8,13) but there is no hint in Luke's narrative that this was what was happening.

Once, in the passage, Luke uses the verb *diakonein* from which we get the transliterated word, 'Deacon'. It describes 'serving' tables. Once he uses the noun *diakonia* to describe the 'ministry' of the Word from which the apostles are saying they must not be diverted. From here Luke proceeds to describe Stephen and Philip, two of the seven, as carrying out the very un-deacon-like functions of preaching, healing, exorcism, etc. So we have to leave the 'Deacon' theory unresolved.

The story of the election of the first people, to whom were delegated the administrative function of handling the daily relief of the needy, is sandwiched between two statements about the growth of the church (Acts 6:1,7). The implication is that if this problem had not been satisfactorily solved, the growth might have stopped. It was as serious as that.

Conservatives and Progressives

In Jerusalem a majority of the people spoke Aramaic and were very conservative about keeping Jewish customs. A significant minority, however, spoke mainly Greek and sat lightly to Jewish customs. They were more influenced by the Greek and Roman world outside Jewry. It was not a recent division. It had built up over three centuries.

The Exile and After

Even earlier, as a judgment from God, Jews had been deported *en masse* to Babylon by King Nebuchadnezzar. After seventy years, a small number returned to Palestine but the majority stayed on in their adopted country (2 Chron.36:17-23). Basically, they made a good contribution to their new situation, even though they remained very much Jews. This gave them a reputation for being good adapters.

When Alexander the Great and his successors wanted to colonize the countries they had conquered and impose the Greek culture on them, they used the Jews to speed this process. Alexander settled 8,000 Jews in Thebes and the Jews formed one third of the population of his new city of Alexandria in Egypt. Large numbers were also brought from Palestine by Ptolemy I and they gradually spread from Egypt, along the whole Mediterranean coast of Africa. Seleucus Nicator removed them by thousands from Babylonia to cities like Antioch and Seleucia. Troubles in Palestine made many more scatter from Palestine until there was hardly a commercial centre in what we call Turkey, Greece and Macedonia in which Jewish communities were not to be found. The vast majority of these Jewish settlers adopted the Greek language.

Over time many of these settlers returned to Palestine for festivals or for family reasons and continued to be Greek speaking and cosmopolitan in their attitudes. People from these Greek speaking groups believed in Jesus and helped to create a minority of the members in the early church.

Widows are Everywhere

The early church in its policy of caring for the needy among them, inevitably found themselves catering for poor widows. In his gospel, Luke shows how destitute widows could be. They could be left without anyone to earn a livelihood (Luke 7:12). They could be denied justice in the courts (Luke 18:1-5). They could forfeit their homes to moneylenders (Luke 20:47). They were left in desperate straits in the absence of any social security system. There were so many widows that it became necessary to have a special distribution of either food or money to relieve their hardships (Acts 6:1). In this context something became apparent that was not so visible when big crowds of believers met. People kept to their own kind and the Greek speaking widows found themselves at the end of the line every day and if the money or the food ran out, they did not receive any. Naturally, they complained and their men folk took up their cause with the leaders. Thus the women initiated a process of great significance for the future of the church.

The Question of Priorities

This was a big enough problem for all twelve of the apostles to become involved. We can imagine the kafuffle as the case was taken to one leader after another who passed the buck until someone said, 'we must stop and look at this seriously.' Before they could settle the relief distribution problem they had to settle the problem of priorities. The apostles should not be handling this kind of problem. They were called to pray and to preach. That should take priority for them. 'So the twelve apostles called the whole group of believers together and said, 'It is not right for us to neglect the preaching of God's word in order to handle finances' (Acts 6:2).

This was a critical realization. There are things that a church can do without. Teaching from the Word of God is not one of them. This teaching is a priority for which someone must assume responsibility in every church or there will be false doctrine, careless living and decline. It was not that they were unwilling to do this service. There just were not enough hours in the day for them to be supervising everything.

Delegation

They decided that the solution was to delegate these tasks. No one, not even an apostle has the gift of omnicompetence. They were going through the same process as Moses when he

took on the leadership of the people through
the desert and had to appoint the seventy elders
to try minor cases (Ex.18:13-27). The Twelve,
in a concerted move, called the whole group
of believers together. It must have been a big
meeting. They set out the qualifications they
saw to be necessary: 'people full of the Holy
Spirit and wisdom.' The word used shows they
were looking for people who had a track record
that everyone could see that showed they were
qualified in these ways. They were not going
to be content with those who volunteered for
the job but lacked proof of competence. Then,
as now, it took no less inspiration from the
Spirit to handle finances and conflict than it
did to preach, teach and pray. Underlying this
requirement of the Holy Spirit was another
truth that emerges from this incident. Both
preaching the Word of God and serving tables
were 'ministry'(Acts 6:3).

Participation
With this understanding they involved the
people by saying, 'So then, brothers and sisters,
you choose seven men among you who are
known to be full of the Holy Spirit and
wisdom, and we will put them in charge of
this matter. We ourselves, then, will give our
full time to prayer and the work of preaching

which has to be our priority.' This is the second time an administrative matter was dealt with by the first believers (See Acts1:15-26). In both cases they involved all the people who were present in some part of the process. It is not yet democracy. The apostles reserved the right to ordain and appoint, but they involved the people and it had the desired effect. 'The whole group was pleased with the apostles' proposal'. They achieved consensus about how to solve the problem. It was not an imposed solution (Acts 6:4,5).

The Candidates
'They chose Stephen, a man full of faith and the Holy Spirit, and Philip, Prochorus, Nicanor, Timon, Parmenas, and Nicolas, a Gentile from Antioch who had earlier been converted to Judaism.' We will have opportunity to learn more detail about Stephen and Philip. The group as a whole has certain features that are worth noticing.

The men all have Greek names. This does not mean that they were all from the group whose widows were complaining. The apostles, Philip and Andrew had Greek names but were conservative Jews from Galilee. It does mean that there was more than an even chance of the malcontents being ready to listen to those who had to solve the problem if some of their own kind were in the leadership.

The last named was Nicolas, a Gentile from Antioch who had earlier been converted to Judaism. Here they seem to have gone beyond the immediate need and made a recommendation that would prove to be valuable when they began to have 'Jewish proselytes' believing in Jesus. The principle is the same. If you want to convince any group in a church that they are really welcome, let them see one or more of their own number taking their place in the leadership. This happened when 'the group presented them to the apostles, who prayed and placed their hands on them' in full view of those assembled (Acts 6:5). It was not long before they were confronted with several Gentiles who had been converted to the Jewish faith and they had a major link with Antioch.

One of the most important decisions we made near the beginning of a multiracial church in Nairobi in 1960 was to appoint a deacon who was Asian and only 21 years of age. It was a sign of our good intentions and it became the most integrated church in town.

The Consequences

'The word of God continued to spread. The number of disciples in Jerusalem grew larger and larger, and a great number of priests accepted the faith' (Acts 6:7). Although this started with the grumbling of widows who were going hungry some days, it was in fact a wake up call, even if less than welcome, to the apostles to change some things that proved to be far reaching. It was the beginning of the major trend that ensured the growth of the church throughout the whole world. It was not a Jewish world. It was a largely Greek speaking world at that time. They built, all unknowingly, the first section of the bridge into that larger world.

We called this chapter, 'Discrimination: a threat to Growth'. We could have called it, 'Disorganization: a Threat to Growth'. Failure to deal with priorities among their tasks or delegation among their ranks would have prevented the great days that followed. We could equally have called it 'Conservatism: a Threat to Growth' and we would have been making a valid point.

Share and Share Alike

Mali in West Africa is a mainly Muslim country. In 1984, there was a widespread famine. In one area there was a string of ten Christian churches that had been static in their membership for many years. Then in 1984 they began to have enquiries from Muslims wanting to become Christians in quite large numbers. The Pastors asked the enquirers, 'We have been here among you for years, why have you become so interested in our gospel now?' They were told, 'When the famine came, we saw you were getting food from abroad. We told ourselves that you would either keep it for yourselves or sell it like the traders for high prices. You did none of these things. You shared it equally with all of us. We need to know the message that makes people behave like that.' The Seven were the first token that there was a message like that.

11

Stephen

A True Martyr

Acts 6:5-8:1

Stephen comes into the book of Acts like a whirlwind. He is suddenly there. He makes a great impact. Then he is gone. We hardly ever hear of him again. The reason is that he was stoned to death in a very short time. He became the first Christian martyr.

Martyrdom has become a very controversial subject with the self-martyrs of Hamas in Palestine. The world calls them suicide bombers because they strap explosives to their body or carry them in a bag and detonate them in public places to kill as many people as possible. These are young Muslims often in their teens, boys and girls who are recruited for this purpose. Their parents may not even know of their intentions. Because they are doing this for Allah, they expect to be rewarded by going straight to paradise where, if men, they would receive seventy virgins and seventy wives in heaven. Their families would receive a cash payment of 12-15,000 US dollars. (*Terror in the Mind of God* by Mark Juergensmeyer p.78) It is interesting to compare Stephen with this contemporary version of martyrdom.

A Powerful Person

There was a problem. Widows who spoke Greek complained that they were not getting as much as the local widows. The Apostles were being drawn into the arguments and distracted from their main job of preaching and praying. They decided on a plan to delegate the responsibility to a group of seven men and asked the people to choose them. Stephen was the first name on the list. Stephen steps into the story as a **practical** man, wise enough to help organize the daily distribution of food to the Greek speaking widows (Acts 6:1-6).

Like Peter and John, he quickly drew on the power of the Holy Spirit within him to perform healings and exorcisms in addition to distributing relief. He was a **spiritual** man. He was opposed by some men who were members of a synagogue of freed slaves who came from provinces in Africa and Asia. Stephen engaged in dialogue with them and won most of the arguments. He was an **intellectual.** He was a

man of many gifts. All this angered his
opponents so much that they bribed some
people to lay false charges against him. As these
charges were about Moses and the Law and
the Temple, they were able to have these
charges brought before the Great Council.
There in the Hall of Stones, in the Temple area,
the Council of seventy men sat in rows
forming a semicircle. The Head of the
Council, the High Priest, with the men who
took notes sat in front, facing them. They
pushed Stephen into the space between the
High Priest and the councillors. The High
Priest asked him, 'Are these charges true?'

Ready to Dialogue

It was a daunting challenge. He had been one
of 'the seven' only days or maybe weeks. Yet
unabashed he launched into his defense. It is a
remarkable speech. He was ready to dialogue
with his accusers. It is the longest speech in
the Acts and nearly twice as long as Peter's
speech at Pentecost. He had wide knowledge.
He gave them his understanding of their own
history. He virtually summarizes the Old
Testament. He talks about Abraham, Isaac,
Jacob, Joseph, Moses, Aaron, Joshua, David,
Solomon, and the prophets. He refers to eleven
of the books in the Old Testament. He

delineates the main facts associated with each of their forefathers that he mentions. It is a tour de force, but it was very conciliatory. He keeps including the Councillors, 'our ancestors,' 'our race' and 'us' (vv.2,8,11,12,19,38,39,44,45).

He keeps to the common ground that they shared, the OT Scriptures. He sticks to the facts and where it helps he makes direct quotations of what God or the prophets said. He shows a wide familiarity with the Bible, that indicates diligent attention to it over a long period. People did not have personal copies of the Scriptures in those days. There were only scrolls, kept in the synagogues or owned by rich Jews. Jesus had said, however, that when they were arrested, they were not to worry about what they should say. The Holy Spirit would give them what to say. This is what happened to Stephen but what a wealth of knowledge he had laid in store for the Holy Spirit to use. Our regular reading of the Bible is always laying up a store for the time when we will need it.

An Honest Person

His speech was wide in its grasp of who God used and where he worked in the past. God was not limited to the Holy Land. He did not limit himself to the Temple. He was everywhere available to all kinds of people. Not only that, he emphasized that there were always people who opposed what God was trying to do. He did not distort their history. This speech was a hinge in events that marks out the gospel as not an exclusively Jewish thing, but a universal gospel that is for the whole world (Acts 7:2-50).

At the end, he speaks very directly to his audience, 'How stubborn you are!' 'How heathen your hearts, how deaf you are to God's message! You are just like your ancestors: you too have always resisted the Holy Spirit! Was there any prophet that your ancestors did not persecute? They killed God's messengers, who long ago announced the coming of his righteous Servant. And now you have betrayed and murdered him. You are the ones who received God's law, that was handed down by angels, yet you have not obeyed it!' (Acts 7:51-53) The Court resented this. They were in denial. They became furious and ground their teeth at him in anger. But **Stephen,** full of the Holy Spirit, looked up to heaven and saw God's glory and Jesus standing at the right-hand side of God. 'Look!' he said. 'I see heaven opened and the Son of Man standing at the right-hand side of God!'

A Winsome Person

Stephen was a calm person. Luke introduced him as a man with grace (Acts 6:8). When he stood at first before the council, unperturbed, with all the shouting going on around him, 'they saw that his face looked like the face of an angel.' At the end even when they were pushing and shoving him to the brow of the cliff where they would push him over and stone him, he was composed enough to see heaven opened and the Son of Man standing by the right hand side of God. He was secure in the love of God. People of great gifts and bold actions are not always like that but it is important to know that Stephen was like this.

I wonder if it was from this remarkable story that the belief arose that Martyrs went straight to heaven. I have not been able to trace the origin of this idea, but this could have been its origin in the minds of unthinking people. What Stephen said he saw in heaven was, 'the Son of Man standing by the right hand side of God.' We have heard this phrase before (Acts2:33,5:31). It was the evidence that God had raised Jesus from death and received him into heaven. Stephen had described Jesus as the new Moses in his defence (Acts 7:37). He was also the Servant who had to suffer for his people (Acts 7:52) and therefore the only one through whom anyone could be saved (Acts 4:12). There is no straight road to heaven from a martyr's or a soldier's death unless that person knows the salvation that only comes from Jesus.

A Violent Reaction

After Stephen's declared vision of Jesus,' With a loud cry the members of the Council covered their ears with their hands. Then they all rushed at him at once, threw him out of the city, and stoned him. The witnesses left their cloaks in the care of a young man named Saul. They kept on stoning **Stephen** as he called out to the Lord, 'Lord Jesus, receive my spirit!' (Acts 7:57-59). Stephen neither initiated or provoked the violence. It came from the Council reacting to his defence against false charges laid against him. They had been at this point before with the apostles and only Gamaliel's intervention had prevented a stoning then. (Acts 5:33) Stephen was passive in all of this as Peter later indicated all Christians must be. If any of you suffers, it must not be because he is a murderer or a thief or a criminal or a meddler in other people's affairs. However, if you suffer because you are a Christian, don't be ashamed of it but thank God that you bear Christ's name (1 Pet.4:15-16).

Forgiving Enemies

There is one more turn that this remarkable martyrdom took. Stephen, in the middle of the stones raining down on him from above, knelt down and cried out in a loud voice, 'Lord! Do not remember this sin against them!' He said this and died (Acts 7:60). Luke clearly sees Stephen's murder as very like the death of Jesus. There were the disputes that stung his opponents to get him arrested. They find false witnesses and bribe them to speak about the destruction of the temple. He is serene in the midst of harassment. The vision of Jesus at the right hand of God is what Jesus, when he was being tried, predicted people would see . He prayed, 'Lord Jesus receive my Spirit' as Jesus had prayed, 'Father, into your hands I commend my spirit.' Finally, he prays, 'Lord do not remember this sin against them!' as Jesus had prayed, 'Father forgive them for they know not what they do'.

A Hamas leader, asked how terrorist violence could be justified, said, 'A Muslim can never call for violence only for love, forgiveness and tolerance!' But he added that, 'if we are aggressed against, if our land is usurped, we must call for hitting the attacker and the aggressor to put an end to the aggression.' (Juergensmeyer p.79) This Stephen did not do, nor his successors in the long train of Christian martyrs. Someone said that 'they out-died their enemies.'

Stephen's Significance

Why does Luke include this long section on Stephen, about whom we hear no more. We have seen one answer. His speech marked the moment when the church could no longer be an exclusive, but a universal gospel.

The second reason is that Stephen's death shows graphically that the Cross was not just the event which brought us salvation. It was a pattern that has to be seen in the life of his followers. Jesus had said that his disciples had to take up their cross and follow him. Here Stephen shows that this was not just a metaphor. It is a real challenge, in his case, quite literal. It is still so. The number of martyrs in 2002 was 164,000. It may not be literal death for us, but the pattern of his dying must be discernible in our lives.

A Modern Martyr

Stephen did something that we are all called to do – to forgive our enemies. In the Idi Amin days in Uganda in 1976, Archbishop Janani Luwum had to pay the ultimate price. The government had summoned a party of Bishops to the Nile Mansion Hotel. After a kind of mock trial of the Archbishop, there was an order of dismissal. The guard said, 'Now you can go home.' But suddenly came fresh orders: 'You Luwum, are wanted in that room by the President.' It was 3.30 p.m. 'He wants to discuss something.'

Festo Kivengere later told journalists, 'I suggested to Bishop Silvanus, as Dean of the Province that he should accompany the Archbishop to meet the President. He went with him to the door, but was ordered away by the security men who said that the President only needed the Archbishop.' Janani turned and smiled at his Bishops. 'I can see the hand of the Lord in this,' he said, and walked away meekly between the armed soldiers. It was his farewell. They never saw him again. He was literally called to lay down his life.

A Fellow Bishop

It was different for Bishop Festo Kivengere. He escaped and worked for the Ugandans who had fled to many countries. On Good Friday 1977 he was alone. He walked up London's teeming Regent Street to the BBC Church, All Souls, Langham Place. He slipped quietly in to join the congregation for the three hour service of meditation on the crucifixion. It was the first time for weeks that he had the opportunity of attending a church as a private individual to pray and to reflect, rather than to minister. Gradually his thoughts settled themselves. He began to wait on God in prayer.

The congregation were invited to reflect on the death of Jesus and how it should affect their lives now. The crucifixion story was read out with the words, 'Father, forgive them for they do not know what they are doing.' Festo began to meditate on the words and, 'Immediately there came, as it were, a great searchlight in my heart. Amin came into the picture and the Lord said, "You owe Amin forgiveness." Festo was shocked, very shocked. Sitting in All Souls, he felt stunned beyond words.

'But, Lord,' he stammered, 'I don't hate this man.' The Lord said, 'Wait a minute. You have been growing hard towards him. Your attitude has been stiffening. Amin is not the loser. You are, Festo. Your hardness will only lead to your own spiritual loss. It will take away your ability to communicate the love of God which is the essence of your ministry and testimony.'

It was quite a shock. Then the Lord said, 'You think it is hard to forgive him? Suppose when the soldiers were putting nails into my hands, one of them had been President Amin.

Would I have said, 'Father, forgive them all except Amin?' It was enough for Festo. In silence he bowed his head. In what he would always consider the high point of his spiritual pilgrimage, he sought the grace that could grant him this level of love and forgiveness. 'When it came, it was fresh air for my tired soul. I knew I had seen the Lord and been released. Love filled my heart.' What about us? Have we forgiven those who have wronged us or ours? If not, it is hurting us and it is hurting God.

The Stephen story had a third purpose – to introduce us to Saul of Tarsus. He was responsible for the lynching. 'The witnesses laid their clothes at the feet of a young man named Saul' (Acts 7:58) He was from Tarsus in Cilicia and may have been among the men who debated with Stephen at their synagogue (Acts 6:9). We can see how much he was influenced by Stephen by comparing his preaching and writing with Stephen's speech.

He was even more influenced by the way Stephen died forgiving his murderers. Later, when he is arguing with the Lord about whether he should stay in Jerusalem or leave, this is how he prayed, 'Lord, these men know that I went from one synagogue to another to imprison and beat those who believed in you.

When the blood of your witness (martyr), Stephen was shed, I stood there giving my approval and guarding the clothes of those who were killing him' (Acts 22:19-20). It was an indelible memory and an irresistible witness to the truth of the gospel that Stephen like Jesus had been able to forgive those who wronged him. In time it overcame him and he began to serve Christ as the Apostle to the Gentiles.

If we can show the same forgiveness to those who wrong us, ours will be a powerful witness also.

The Collect for St. Stephen's Day:

Heavenly Father, give us grace in all our sufferings for the truth to follow the example of your first martyr Stephen: that we may also look to him who was crucified and pray for those who persecute us; through Jesus Christ our Lord.

12

Philip: 'The Surprise Evangelist'

Acts 8:4-13, 26-40; 21:8-11

The stoning of Stephen, was a sad day for the
infant church. The whole might of Jewish
authority was ranged against them. 'That very
day the church in Jerusalem began to suffer
cruel persecution. All the believers, except the
apostles, were scattered throughout the
provinces of Judea and Samaria. Some devout
men buried Stephen, mourning for him with
loud cries' (Acts 8:1-2). It was a very different
funeral from those of Ananias and Sapphira.
It was complicated by the fact that thousands
of people had to make immediate arrangements
to leave the city if they did not want to be
arrested themselves.

Oddly, the only ones who did not leave
were the apostles who must have gone
underground. We do not hear of them
preaching in Jerusalem again. The next one to
preach in Jerusalem was Saul of Tarsus, but
they tried to kill him. He had to be spirited

out of the city and dispatched to Tarsus, his own home town. For some reason that episode took the pressure off and they had some respite throughout the whole country (Acts 9:29-31).

A Mission by Refugees

What a devastating experience it must have been for those who became instant refugees. Where were they to go? How long was it going to be for? How could they maintain themselves cut off from their means of livelihood or the generosity of the church? The election of 'the seven' must have seemed irrelevant a very short time after they had been put in place. Any continuance of their work must have been clandestine in the extreme.

Yet the refugees did not lose their nerve. 'The believers who were scattered went everywhere, preaching the message' (Acts 8:4). It shows how incredibly confidant they must have been in the gospel. Among them would be some who had been included in the seventy-two people that Jesus sent out two by two in his lifetime (Luke 10:1-12). They had first hand experience of how to go about this and a clear memory of the instructions Jesus had given them on that occasion. Some have suggested that Philip, one of the seven, might have been in that category.

Some of the major carriers of the gospel today are the 'Diasporas'. A recent Ph.D. thesis has shown that it was the refugees from North Korea that gave rise to the hugely successful mega church phenomenon in South Korea. The largest and fastest growing churches in London are made up of immigrants to the country. This is replicated in other countries too. We are likely to see the gospel increasingly travel along the highways of migration in the future.

The Instant Evangelist

Philip is the only named person in the New Testament who is actually called an 'evangelist'. He is not Philip the Apostle from Bethsaida (John 1:44). The word 'evangelist' occurs only in two other places and is a general description (Eph.4:11, 1 Tim 3:8,12). 'Evangel' and the words derived from it present problems. The English word is a transliteration of the Greek, (*evangelion*) not a translation.

Transliterations have the disadvantage that people tend to make them mean what they want them to mean. 'Baptism' is another transliteration and look at the controversies it has started. Every denomination in every country and language continues to use the transliteration to describe a great diversity of practice. William Carey, the first Baptist Missionary to India fell out with the Bible Society because he wanted to translate 'to baptize' as 'to immerse' in the many Indian languages into which he translated the New Testament. The Bible Society won in the end and the ambiguity of 'baptism' was upheld!

Today there is considerable confusion and disagreement about what 'evangelism' is and is not. 'Evangelical' tends to mean a different thing in different countries. 'Evangelization' for many is the preferred concept to 'Evangelism'. One interesting fact that is itself a commentary on the passions aroused about evangelism is that it is an expression not much used in the New Testament. John does not use it at all either in his gospel or in his letters. He prefers 'witness'.

Perhaps Philip can help us in this. He is not the only one to be called an evangelist in the New Testament. Luke uses the expressions related to the word 'evangel' more in his story than anywhere else in the New Testament. Philip is a good model when we want to see what authentic evangelism is.

Spontaneous Evangelism

Philip found himself unexpectedly in Samaria. In this way the prediction of Jesus that they would be witnesses in Samaria was fulfilled (Acts1:8). Philip had hoped still to be looking after the distribution of relief to the poor widows in Jerusalem. The day before he was doing just that no doubt with a great sense of responsibility in the task. Then he was on the run. His task was abruptly taken from him and he was in Samaria. We do not know if it was a strange place to him or not. In any case he just set about doing there what they had all been doing in Jerusalem, witnessing about Jesus, the Messiah who had saved them. He naturally continued to do the same and found he was drawing crowds of people, so, in the absence of Peter or another Apostle to step into the breach, to his great surprise, he became the preacher.

Mass Evangelism

Samaria was a district as well as a city. We do not know where Philip preached. It could have been near the village of Sychar where Jesus had his encounter with the woman of Samaria (John 4:-41). Perhaps it was near where one or more of the lepers live whom Jesus healed of their leprosy (Luke17:10-19). In either case they would have known something about Jesus of Nazareth. Wherever it was, 'Philip preached the Messiah to the people there. The crowds paid close attention to what Philip said, as they listened to him and saw the miracles that he performed. Evil spirits came out from many people with a loud cry, and many paralysed and lame people were healed.' In that atmosphere we are not surprised to learn that there was great joy in that city (Acts:8:5-8). Luke uses here a word that implies the presence of crowd psychology. There are times when this is an important beginning as was the case in the early ministry of Jesus, when the multitudes flocked to hear him. They believed Philip's message about the good news of the Kingdom of God and about Jesus Christ, and they were baptized, both men and women (Acts 8:12). This was carefully followed up, however, by the visit of Peter and John who brought what had been lacking in the people's first encounter with the message (Acts 8:14-25). Philip was clearly willing to have his limited experience supplemented by the greater wisdom of these two apostles.

Personal Evangelism
Philip was just as happy to leave all the excitement of the new movement in Samaria and be sent out into the desert to meet a single person traveling back from Jerusalem to Ethiopia. He sat in his chariot with the high

ranking Eunuch and preached Jesus to him from the passage in Isaiah, that, in the providence of God he happened to be reading. The man was convinced by what he said and asked to baptized. Philip baptized him and he went on his way. The Ethiopian was also full of joy out there on the desert road. And Philip moved on to other places and eventually settled down in the port city of Caesarea.

Appropriate to the Context

Samaritan religion had been a very hybrid affair from its beginning. 'They worshipped the LORD, but they also worshipped their own gods according to the customs of the countries from which they had come' (2 Kings 17:33). They had held on to the Pentateuch or the Books of the Law. They were also expecting Messiah to come (John 4:25), so Philip preached the Messiah to them. Currently, they were under the spell of a kind of Shaman who was into all kinds of occult practices. In that context, the healings and exorcisms that Philip performed were vital to get the attention of the people.

People ask today why about 75 per cent of the Protestants in Latin America are Pentecostal. One answer is that they take seriously the syncretistic nature of the

Catholicism of the people and their involvement in spiritism and other occult practices. People receive deliverance from very real powers through the ministry of Pentecostal pastors and evangelists.

The Ethiopian Treasurer, on the other hand, was a Jew or a Jewish convert who was on his way back from Jerusalem where he had been worshipping in the Temple. He owned a rather expensive parchment scroll of the prophet Isaiah and had it open at Isaiah 53. Very naturally Philip asked him if he understood what he was reading. This was a passage that Jesus more than once had applied to himself (Mark 14:49, Luke 22:37) so Philip knew that, if the man was willing, he could use this to preach about Jesus' death on the cross to him. The man was totally open and the witness was completed with a positive result. This is likely to have been the channel through which the gospel first reached Ethiopia.

Biblically Based Evangelism

The scattered believers, of whom Philip was one, went everywhere preaching **the word** or **the message.** We have seen how much the preaching of Peter and Stephen was based on the Scriptures. Philip, for all that he was catapulted into the role of evangelist, knew the importance of this and made his presentation to the Ethiopian seeker and stuck to the scripture he found him already reading.

Continuous Evangelism

After he left the Ethiopian he went on to Caesarea, and on the way he preached the Good News in every town. Twenty years later, he is still there, now married with four daughters who had the gift of prophecy. When Luke and Paul and the others visit him, they find Philip is still known as 'the evangelist'. It is a sad fact that for many of us, the longer we have known Jesus, the less we are articulate in speaking of him to others. Part of it is that we find all our friends in the church and have few real friendships with people who do not already know the Lord. Philip is a reminder that we are never too old to witness. It is more than likely that it was from his own mouth that Luke got these two stories that he included in Acts 8.

Life is changing for older people. They are living longer not only in the West. They can often sense a lack of purpose in having retired without their daily work to go out to. In Japan, where the big companies squeezed so much out of their loyal employees, retired people are proving more open to a gospel that gives them a new identity and a new purpose in life even after sixty-five. Philip is a model for us not only when he was younger, but even in his later life.

13

Simon Magus: A Power Encounter

Acts 8:9-24

A History of Syncretism

In Samaria, Philip had one convert that became
a problem. Knowing about the Samaritans is
very important if you want to understand
many things in the Gospels, especially Luke,
and the Acts. They were a hybrid community.
They date back seven hundred years to when
Israel was taken into exile to Assyria. The
Assyrians were the first to use deportation and
the resettlement of peoples to pacify the lands
that they conquered. The King of Assyria took
the people of Israel to Assyria and replaced
them with people from five of his other cities.
They all came with different gods and set up
their shrines. They were having difficulties
settling, so the Emperor sent back one of
Israel's priests to teach them how to worship
the Lord, Jehovah. This resulted in a great
mish-mash of religions from all over the place.
It is summed up with the words, 'So they

worshipped the Lord, but they also worshipped their own gods, according to the customs of the countries from which they had come' (2 Kings 17:33) This was the ultimate in syncretism. Syncretism is a mix and match approach where you incorporate bits from several religions to make a new 'product'.

This community has had astonishing longevity. Some of them are still there. I have seen and talked with them. They showed us the Samaritan Pentateuch and I have a slide to prove it. Relations between them and the Jews were never good. Jesus starts a new chapter in Jewish Samaritan relations, in spite of the deadly hostility between the two peoples (John 4:1-41, Luke10:25-37, 17:11-19).

We are not surprised to find that Samaria was an early stop for the Christians, who were chased out of Jerusalem by persecution. Jesus had said they were to be witnesses in Samaria (Acts1:8), Philip found himself in Samaria and so became the evangelist. He preached the Messiah to the people. The crowds paid close attention to what Philip said as they listened to him and saw the miracles that he performed. Evil spirits came out from many people with a loud cry and many paralysed and lame people were healed. So there was great joy in that city (Acts 8:4-8).

A Local Shaman

Given the syncretistic history of the Samaritans we are not surprised that they had a man named Simon, who lived there who, for some time, had astounded the Samaritans with his sorcery. He claimed that he was someone great and everyone in the city, from all classes of society, paid close attention to him. 'He is that power of God', known as The Great Power, they said. But when they believed Philip's message about the good news of the Kingdom of God and about Jesus the Messiah, they were baptized, both men and women. Simon himself also believed; and after being baptized, he stayed close to Philip and was astounded when he saw the great wonders and miracles that were being performed' (Acts 8:9-13). So far, so good! I am sure that Philip felt it was a wonderful evidence of God's working that such a prominent person had come to believe in Jesus.

For Simon there was another wonder still to come. The move to Samaria had been sudden and unanticipated. Philip was not an Apostle. The Apostles had decided to stay on in Jerusalem in spite of the persecution. Soon they got the news about what was happening in Samaria and for some reason 'they sent Peter and John to them. When they arrived, they

prayed for these new believers that they might
receive the Holy Spirit, for the Holy Spirit had
not yet come down on any of them; they had
only been baptized in the name of the Lord
Jesus. So Peter and John laid their hands on
them and they received the Holy Spirit' (Acts
8:14-17).

An Understandable Mistake

'Simon saw that the Spirit had been given to
the believers when the apostles placed their
hands on them.' They may have spoken in
tongues. This was something else. He was
impressed. He had never seen this before. He
wanted to add this power to his already
significant powers. 'So he offered money to
Peter and John.' This is the animistic
approach. When you want to draw on the
occult powers, money or some other gift has
to change hands. It was just like Saul's approach
to Samuel, the seer to seek help in finding his
lost donkeys (1 Sam.9:7-8). 'Give this power
to me too, so that anyone that I place my hands
on might receive the Holy Spirit.'

Simon saw what Peter and John were doing
as just an extension of the things he practiced
himself. Sometimes the phenomena that follow
the preaching of the gospel are similar to those
seen in other religions, cults or movements.

They look the same. They appeal to the same psychic capacities that can be present in people of a particular temperament. Anthropology shows that all the phenomena we read of in the NT are found in other contexts. The difference is that they are differently motivated and directed, if they are from the Holy Spirit. Here lies the danger in much of the New Age scene. We already noted that Peter implies the danger of this confusion between the word of Christ, the New Moses and what comes from mediums, etc. (Chapter 5. p.64) We shall see this clash later in Paul's missions.

An Unreconstructed Animist

Simon's words show that he was still an unreconstructed animist. Peter saw this straight away. He answered him rather roughly. 'May your money perish with you, because you thought you could buy the gift of God with money. You have no part or share in our work, because your heart is not right in God's sight.' It was tough talk and he kept going. 'Repent then of this evil plan of yours and pray to the Lord to forgive you for thinking such a thing as this. For I see that you are full of bitter envy and a prisoner of sin' (Acts 8:18-23).

This is strong language. What a day that was to be alive, when discernment was acute and financial scams were nipped in the bud before they got going! It was the same with Ananias and Sapphira, four chapters earlier. They too were after something on the side financially and pretended that they were really Kosher Christians in their giving. The same Peter was scathing to them also (Acts 5:1-11).

Simon was not dealt with as drastically. He was not an insider. He was just at the threshold of the kingdom. He envied the gifts of the two apostles. This bitter envy locked him into the prison of self seeking insincerity. He seemed to get the message. 'Simon said to Peter and John, "Please pray to the Lord for me so that none of these things you spoke of will happen to me"' (Acts 8:24).

It would appear that he was not sincere. We hear no more of him in the New Testament. But he comes many times into the literature of the Apostolic Age and later. He is called Simon the Heresiarch or the Arch Heretic who was a trouble to the churches for a long time and in many places. Some say that he was the origin of the Gnostic heresy that afflicted the church for so long.

The Temptations of Power

'He is that power of God, known as "The Great Power"' they said about Simon. 'Give me this power!' was his request to Peter and John. The gospel is not about wielding power or seeking ego trips (Mark 10:42-43). Where power is concerned, we are to be channels of God's power and it is to be demonstrated in such a away that God is honoured and not we. Jesus, in the Sermon on the mount, warned, 'When judgment day comes, many will say, Lord! Lord! In your name we prophesied. By your name we drove out many demons and performed many miracles! Then I will say to them, "I never knew you. Get away from me you wicked people."' It is those who do the will of the father who are welcomed. This indicates that it is possible to demonstrate the possessions of powers even in the name of Jesus and have no part in his Kingdom.

The Temptations of Money

Simon has given his name as a word in English and in other languages also. 'Simony' means being involved in giving or getting a position in the church in return for money. In fifteenth century Europe, kings, emperors and popes bestowed bishoprics and other benefices in return for large contributions to their treasuries. There is a story of an Austrian Duke who wanted an office in the church for a relative of his. He offered the Pope of the time 10,000 gold ducats for the privilege, and said that this was 1,000 ducats for each of the ten commandments. The Pope reminded the duke that there were twelve apostles. The duke's rejoinder was that there were only Seven deadly sins. They settled for 10,000 ducats. That is 'simony'.

The Prison of Bitterness

Peter discerned that, underneath Simon's bold exterior, there was a sad story of disappointment, hate and anger that left a sediment of bitterness at the bottom of this man's personality. He was a driven man. He was caught in the toils of years of resentment and had to keep adding to his ability to control people, by whatever means. His room for moral manoeuvre was now very limited. Peter urged him to 'pray God that if perhaps, the thought of thine heart may be forgiven thee (Acts 8:22 AV). There is a fear in Peter that he may already have gone too far in his chosen ways.

Our Motivation

People with great ministries and impressive Christian credentials can be bogus. The tell-tale sign of the counterfeit is that they are in it for themselves, the power they can wield over others, and the gains they can make financially. They want to dominate the lives of others. When our service for Christ means more to us that it does to those whom we serve, we are in the wrong place. When we have a basically animistic approach to faith, seeking a quid pro quo from God, we do not yet have the essence of the matter.

I recall seeing this in Africa even with young people. Students became very religious and attended Chapel and the Christian Union meetings in large numbers at exam times. The attitude was that if I do the right thing by God, he will do the right thing by me. That is animism. That is not Christian faith. Yes, there are promises of God that we can claim by faith but the criterion is that they are fulfilled for the glory of God and not just to gratify our personal whims.

We need to note the syncretistic nature of the people among whom Simon lived and assume that he grew up with ideas that militated against both the law of God in the Old Testament and the gospel in the New. It made him hungry for power. It made him want to adopt Christian faith as just another weapon in his armoury of sorcery.

In the late eighties, I was in Ecuador in South America. One Saturday we were in a strange market. On sale were little models of washing machines and other household gadgets, automobiles, houses, office and farm equipment and even fake US Dollars. It was a festival of the goddess Eko. The people believed that if they purchased items that symbolized their wishes for the coming year as close to midday as they could, these wishes would be fulfilled. Later in the afternoon we went to a Catholic Church in the city. We saw a long queue of people clutching the things they had bought and waiting their turn to place them in the shrine of a saint to pray for their wishes to be fulfilled.

Later in trying to discover the origins of such a practice, I read something very significant. It seems that when the Roman Catholic Church colonized South America 400 years earlier, they had a formula for dealing with the customs of the local people whom they were converting to the Christian faith. If the customs were regarded as heresy, they had to be stamped out by force. If, however, they could be classified as superstition, they could be left for education to deal with them in time. The result was the Christo-paganism that still exists all over Latin America centuries later. It is fatal to try just to add Jesus to the faith or religion that you already have.

This is a constant temptation in India, where Hindus are willing to place Jesus alongside their millions of other gods. It happens also in Africa and is often in evidence in the fact that Christians resort to the witch doctor for help to attain the things they feel they need, like health or a job or even the success of their football team.

The case of Simon Magus is a permanent warning that you cannot just add Jesus to the faith or religious practice that you already have. He is unique and he has to be supreme in our lives and our loyalties.

14

The Ethiopian Official: How Can I Understand?

Acts 8:26-40

The circle gets wider all the time. Now it is a high official from Ethiopia and it is not the Apostles who are driving the process. It is not even Philip the evangelist to Samaria. In the middle of the dramatic response to the gospel there, Philip is visited by an angel.

A Chariot on a Desert Road
The angel instructs Philip, 'Get ready and go south to the road that goes from Jerusalem to Gaza.' Samaria is about 35 miles north of Jerusalem and Gaza is about 50 miles South West of Jerusalem. Philip is on foot, so we are talking about three or more days journey – a long walk without a specific destination.

It is only when he is well on the road to Gaza that he got further instructions. On the road there was a high official from Ethiopia travelling in a chariot (probably covered) back to his own country south of Egypt. He was in

the service of the Queen or the Queen mother
of Ethiopia and had been made or had become
a eunuch for that purpose. He was in charge
of the Royal Treasury.

A Tourist to the Temple

He had been to Jerusalem to worship God in
the temple. This means that he was either a
Jew or in process of being converted to
Judaism. It is possible that he was a Jew whose
family had been used by Alexander the Great
or his successors in colonizing the countries
they had conquered. We do not know how
much they integrated. We do not know if he
was black, even if it would be nice to think so.
Every Diaspora Jew longed to visit Jerusalem
at least once in his lifetime and this may have
been this man's great occasion.

Herod's Temple was a magnificent place to
visit. It has been completed only relatively
recently and ranked as one of the wonders of
the world of that period. It is interesting to
speculate who, in Jerusalem might have
received him and shown him round the
wonders of the Temple, the Hippodrome and
the other buildings erected by Herod the Great.
It could have been other Ethiopians. Could it
have been Pontius Pilate, Herod, the High
Priests or some of their officials? There are

no indications that it was any kind of official visit.

We are not told if he came up for a festival, what time of year it was or how long he stayed. We do not know whether he had heard of the new religious movement centred around Jesus of Nazareth or the measures taken by the authorities to stamp it out. From the atmosphere that Luke portrays, it would hardly seem likely that he had not heard of it. If we follow Josephus, the Jewish historian, it is probably less likely that he had heard of the apostles but would have heard about Jesus, his crucifixion and alleged resurrection.

A Valuable Souvenir

We do know that he was carrying a copy of the scroll of the Isaiah Scriptures. We do not know if he bought it as a souvenir of his visit or had been given it as a gift. Why did he want a scroll? Why did he choose Isaiah or had he bought all the scrolls but had taken out this one to peruse on his journey home? Had someone told him of that reference in Isaiah 11:11 where God's promised King would come and recover the remnant of his people from 'Cush', the Biblical name for Ethiopia?

In any case, he was reading aloud much further on in the scroll, while bumping along in his chariot. Philip was prompted by the Spirit to approach the vehicle. He ran over and to his surprise heard this distinguished foreign stranger reading aloud from Isaiah 53, one of the passages they had been learning was a prophecy about Messiah (Acts 3:18, 7:52). Jogging alongside the chariot, Philip asked its occupant, 'Do you understand what you are reading?' The official replied, 'How can I understand unless someone explains it to me?' And he invited Philip to climb up and sit in the vehicle with him (Acts 8:31).

An Unexpected Companion

Philip climbed into the chariot and the man read aloud the lines he had reached in the Greek translation scroll.

> 'Like a sheep that is taken to be slaughtered, like a lamb that makes no sound when its wool is cut off, he did not say a word.
> He was humiliated, and justice was denied him. No one will be able to tell about his descendants, because his life on earth has come to an end.'

He then asked Philip, 'Tell me, of whom is the prophet saying this? Of himself or of someone else?'

It was a key question. Up until that time, no Jews had thought that this was a statement about the coming Messiah. The texts they recognized were all about an imperial, triumphant Messiah. The idea of him being a Servant or having to suffer was far from their thoughts. The words were in any case obscure because of their prophetic and poetic form. Fortunately, Philip, though not a Rabbi, knew the passage and told him it was a passage about the Servant of God who was to come and who had to suffer, not for his own sins, but for the sins of everyone.

No doubt Philip would point back to the previous verse, 'All of us were like sheep that were lost, each of us going his own way; but the LORD made the punishment fall on him, the punishment all of us deserved.' This he would explain was why he was crucified.

Then he would go further down on the scroll to a later place where it said, 'And so he will see his descendants; he will live a long life, and through him my purpose will succeed. After a life of suffering, he will again have joy; he will know that he did not suffer in vain.' Philip would explain that this was a foreshadowing of the triumph of his being raised from death and raised to God's right hand. Luke says that he told him the good news about Jesus. (It says literally, 'He evangelized Jesus to him.')

We have to imagine the rest of the conversation, how long it lasted, what it contained and how the official and his unexpected passenger related to each other. It obviously went well and the man was persuaded that the interpretation was not only true but applied to him.

An Abrupt Goodbye

They noticed they had come to an oasis in the desert and the Ethiopian said, 'Here is some water. What is to keep me from being baptized?' The official ordered the carriage to stop, and both Philip and the official went down into the water, and Philip baptized him. When they came up out of the water, as quickly as Philip had arrived, he disappeared. Nothing daunted the Ethiopian – he continued on his way, full of joy.

The Word of God and how it Works.

Clearly the Ethiopian was a seeker after God, whether a Jew or a Proselyte. He had made the 1,500 mile journey up the Nile and through the desert to worship in Jerusalem, the place where God had said his people were to worship him. On the return journey he is delving into the Scriptures for himself. He wants to understand them. He is open to receive help for that purpose even from a stranger. When he sees the heart-warming truths he is ready to act on them and commit himself to a lifelong following of Jesus whom he saw in Isaiah.

His experience is instructive and epitomizes what has been implied in Acts up to this point. There are four elements in coming to an understanding of the Word of God. There is

· what the text actually says.
· the open and enquiring mind of the person.
· the illumination of the Holy Spirit
· usually a human interpreter.

The 'Word' (*logos*) is ultimately a spoken word. With the truth of the gospel, God has given preachers, teachers, evangelists, and prophets (Eph.4:11). What God has given, we should not try to do without.

Later Paul described it, 'Faith comes by hearing and hearing by the word of God.' (Rom.10:17) Just as the lame man was a case history of the signs and wonders that abounded in the earliest church, so the Ethiopian Official is a case history of how a person is evangelised. Let me give you a modern example.

A young man from Germany came to Kenya, at the age of nineteen. He had been confirmed in the Lutheran Church in Germany. For this purpose he had learned verses from the Bible and had to attend church for two years. That was the tradition at that time. It was also the tradition to leave the church after confirmation and to return only for weddings, baptisms and burials.

Before leaving Germany a strange longing for God had somehow grown up in him. He started attending church again but the connection between what was said or sung and life did not materialize. Church was church and life was life. This continued also during the first months in Kenya. Then he was invited by a business contact to accompany him to Church.

The pastor preached from the book of Isaiah. Three things attracted him. The preacher had an experience with God that was alive. He dug truth out of the text and applied it to life. That made a difference to him . He was not convicted of sin, nor did he see the plan of salvation on that day. He just felt that God and life were finally meeting. He came back for more and got more. He and pastor started from scratch. He was given a New Testament, and started reading.During that first contact with what he called 'real Christianity' he was exposed to scripture in two ways.

Every Sunday he heard the Bible expounded and privately he started reading the New Testament. These had completely different effects: The truth from the sermons, he could, perceive and apply to his life. His own private readings produced more questions than answers. These questions he solved in private meetings. In these meetings he felt he was not only learning theology, why this and why that, he was encouraged to trust in the Word of God. He had looked on the Bible as a book of stories but the pastor trusted it.

As he started trusting the Word he began experiencing its truth himself. It simply worked. In this way he brought many parts of his life under the influence of the Word . At the end of a long development, and by then in Venezuela, he went on his knees, asked God for forgiveness and handed his life over to Jesus. In his coming to faith in Christ, it was not scripture alone; he needed a teacher to help him understand and apply and then he felt its power himself and was grateful to the teacher.

15

Saul of Tarsus: The Ravager of the Church

Acts 8:1-3, 9:1-30

A Reign of Terror

Back in Jerusalem, terror continued to rage. Its instigator was Saul, a Pharisee from the city of Tarsus in what we know as South East Turkey. He had been a student of Gamaliel but had imbibed none of his mildness (See chapter 8). In this own words, 'I was circumcised when I was a week old. I am an Israelite by birth, of the tribe of Benjamin, a pure-blooded Hebrew. As far as keeping the Jewish Law is concerned, I was a Pharisee... As far as a person can be righteous by obeying the commands of the Law, I was without fault' (Phil.3:5-6). He appeared out of nowhere with a fervour and fury for persecuting the followers of Jesus of Nazareth that has seldom been equalled. In retrospect, he uses language of himself that indicated his behaviour was almost manic (Acts 26:11).

In general, what he did is described by Luke and by himself in words that in other places were used to describe the scorched earth policy pursued by an invading army (Acts 8:3, 9:21, Gal.1:13,23). It was cruel persecution. He went from house to house dragging out both men and women and throwing them into jail (Acts8:3). He maintained an uninterrupted barrage of violent threats of murder against the followers of the Lord (Acts 9:1), he persecuted to the death the people who followed this way (Acts 22:4), both directly and by casting his vote when the death penalty was called for in the Council. Where he could, he tried to force them to deny their faith and blaspheme (Acts 26:10-11).

An Ominous Silence

He was successful. The Christians fled Jerusalem in droves (Acts 8:1). There were no more preachings or wonders in Solomon's Porch; no more crowds gathered in the streets to wait the passing shadow of Peter and John; no more gatherings assembled in the house of Mary the mother of John Mark; there was no more public distribution of relief to the widows. If the Christians met, they met in anxious secrecy and small numbers as they had in the days before the Ascension with the doors closed for fear of the Jews. The heady times of their initial popularity with the people were a mere dream. They became forerunners of a great multitude of suffering Christians down the centuries. Like them also generation after generation has found that the blood of the martyrs became the seed of the church.

Terror Today

Laskar Jihad (Islamic Holy War Army) first came to attention on 6 April 2000 when Islamic extremists gathered for a rally in Jakarta, the capital of Indonesia. They called for a Jihad (holy war) against the Christians of the Maluku islands. They announced that 10,000 armed militants were in training and would be sent to launch an attack against the Christians on Good Friday, 2000. By early May at least 1,000 had made their way to Maluku and many more followed.

Over 1,000 people were butchered in a single raid. In another, 200 were killed and their bodies horribly mutilated. In June some 200 Christians, sheltering in a church were attacked with machetes. The church was then surrounded and set on fire. At least 100 Christians died in the blaze. In another incident, three children were tied up and dragged to their deaths behind a speeding car.

At Duma, Halmahera island, 300 Christian women and girls were abducted. They are believed to have been taken to another island and raped.

By the end of the year 2000 at least 455 churches had been destroyed, and 5,000 Christians killed. As I write this in June 2002, steps look like being taken to end this tragedy but are being resisted vigorously by Laskar Jihad. This was the kind of atmosphere in which the believers found themselves in Jerusalem when Saul was at work.

Exporting Terror

Saul decided to go after the scattering believers. The High Priest and the Council had jurisdiction over Jews in synagogues in foreign cities, so he secured authorization to pursue his vendetta against Christians in Damascus, 150 miles away. He knew he would still find them in the synagogues. He was authorized to arrest them, both men and women and bring them back in chains to Jerusalem (Acts 22:4-5). Threatening and murderous was the atmosphere which Saul breathed and in which he lived (Acts 9:1). Why would a man behave in such a sadistic way?

An Unbelievable Transformation

He does give us some information about his makeup. He speaks about not being able to control his behaviour. He describes a time in his life when he was really alive, but then he died (Rom.7:9). He attributes this inward death to his becoming aware of God's Law which had the effect of provoking him to do what the Law forbade. We may get a clue from the question that Jesus put to him in his vision. Why is it me you are persecuting? Were there others against whom he had a deep anger because of some betrayal in the past? Was he in fact so inwardly driven by resentment against others that he had to take it out on someone and the Christians became his immediate targets?

Josef Stalin, in 1936-1938 was responsible for one of the worst reigns of terror that the world has ever known. His biographer says, 'The boy grew up in a violent and bitter household. He was beaten by both parents. It is clear he underwent an early and intense hardening, quite sufficient to inaugurate the hatred of any authority other than his own that would mark him to his death.'

Physical factors contributed to his sense of resentment and inferiority. The young Stalin was ugly. His eyes were unpleasantly close together. His face was pitted by smallpox. Above all, he was short; five feet four inches, handicapped with a stiff left elbow and deformed with the second and third toes on his left foot joined, a conspicuous handicap when children played barefoot. He had enough physical shortcomings to give him the bitter drive of a Shakespearian bastard. (*Stalin* by Alex de Jonge p.24)

We wonder if there was anything in his earlier history like this that precipitated Saul into his ferocious cruelty to the followers of Jesus. There is a document from the first century that describes Paul as bald headed, bow legged, strongly built, small in size with meeting eyebrows with a rather large nose. When we read this we wonder.

And yet the more remarkable thing is that having started out as the monster he was, he was changed. He later became such a giant of a man, ready to suffer himself without complaint almost everything he had perpetrated on others. We do not know that they ever tried to make him blaspheme, but to the last dregs of lonely martyrdom he drank the bitter cup of persecution. He says, 'I have been in prison; I have been whipped; I have been near death often. Five times I was given the thirty-nine lashes by the Jews; three times I was whipped

by the Romans; and once I was stoned. I have
been in three shipwrecks, and once I spent
twenty-four hours in the water. I have been in
danger from floods, robbers and from fellow-
Jews and Gentiles. There have been dangers
in the cities, the wilds, on the high seas, and
from false friends. There has been work and
toil; I have gone without sleep; I have been
hungry and thirsty; I have often been without
enough food, shelter, or clothing. He got as
good as he gave – and more (2 Cor.11:23-27).
How could he become so different?

Did the forgiving spirit of Stephen start
goading him towards what he needed to do
with his own hurts? Did this make him lash
out blindly, in a fury of persecution, at
everyone who was like Stephen? We cannot
answer these questions with any certainty but
we can marvel that such a change took place
when Jesus revealed himself within him. Saul
reached Damascus a changed man and he never
did complete his mission. What happened to
it we do not know. The story of how Saul was
changed will be told in a later book.

The Persecutor Disappears

As far as the church in Jerusalem is concerned,
Saul just disappeared for the best part of three
years. No doubt they heard reports or rumours

that he had come to faith in Jesus whom he
had persecuted. That did not affect them. They
knew nothing of the fact that he had retired to
Arabia presumably to come to terms with the
impact of his dramatic conversion (Gal.1:17).
All they knew was that he was no longer
masterminding the persecution in Jerusalem

The Return

In the third year after he left for Damascus,
'Saul went back to Jerusalem and tried to join
the disciples. But they would not believe that
he was a disciple, and they were all afraid of
him.' (Acts 9:26) We can understand their
reservations. Many of the believers were
widows or orphans or maimed in body as a
result of his activities.

We can also understand what a great
disappointment and discouragement it was for
Saul, to be rejected out of hand when he was
so anxious to make amends for all the damage
he had done. After all, he had not rushed back.
Time had indeed passed but bitter memories
die hard.

There was one person who was prepared
to see it differently. We have met him before.
He was Joseph, a Levite from Cyprus, a
generous man to whom the Apostles had given
the high honour of calling him 'Barnabas',

which means 'One who encourages'. (Acts 4:36) He lived up to his name.

Barnabas came to Saul's help. He listened to his story and then took him to the apostles. He explained to them how Saul had seen the Lord on the road and that the Lord had spoken to him. He also told them how boldly Saul had preached in the name of Jesus in Damascus. And so Saul stayed with them for two weeks. He wanted information from Peter and he also met James the Lord's brother but did not mix much with any others (Gal.1:18-19). In this short time he set out to go all over Jerusalem, preaching boldly in the name of the Lord as he had done in Damascus on his way back. He also talked and disputed with the Greek-speaking Jews, of the kind that Stephen had been up against, but they tried to kill Saul also.

More Waiting

When the believers found out about this, they took Saul to Caesarea and sent him back home to Tarsus. He did not go willingly. He was impatient to start where he had left off and set the record straight. While he was praying in the Temple, however, he had a vision, in which he saw the Lord, who said to him, 'Hurry and leave Jerusalem quickly, because the people here will not accept your witness about me.'

'Lord,' he answered, 'they know very well that I went to the synagogues and arrested and beat those who believe in you. And when your witness Stephen was put to death, I myself was there, approving of his murder and taking care of the cloaks of his murderers.' 'Go!' the Lord said to him, 'for I will send you far away to the Gentiles.' He still had some more waiting in obscurity to face.

How differently churches today might have handled the newly converted Saul! The church today would not have had the patience to endure first his retreat to Arabia or his second to Tarsus. We would have wanted to display him like a trophy, using his notoriety as a draw to bring others to meetings or to TV screens that they might hear the gospel from him. That was not the NT way. The fact of persecution, of course, made a difference. Yet, today, it is likely that such a person in a situation of persecution, would flee his own country and become a celebrity in a country where there was no danger and raise money or prayer support for the people he had left behind.

We are seldom wise when we ignore the word of Paul himself in the New Testament, 'Be in no hurry to lay hands on anyone in dedication to the Lord's service.' The Parable of the sower indicates the time and care it takes,

'The seeds that fell in good soil stand for those who hear the message and retain it in a good and obedient heart, and they persist until they bear fruit.' (Luke 8:15)

16

Aeneas and Dorcas: Business as usual

Acts 9:31-43

A Respite

After Saul had been sent back to Tarsus, there was a lull in the persecution of the church throughout Judea, Galilee, and Samaria. It is remarkable how widely the gospel had been established in the four years (plus or minus) between Pentecost and Saul's return home. At least two of these years had been filled with cruel persecution and destabilization. Yet, it only poured fuel on the fire of witness to which the early believers were committed. Throughout the three main districts of Palestine the church was strengthened in faith and grew in numbers (Acts 9:31).

There were other political factors that contributed to the lessening of the persecution. The Roman Emperor, Caligula, tried to pursue an insane policy of erecting statues to himself everywhere including synagogues. He even determined to erect a huge one in the Temple in Jerusalem. This evoked passionate demonstrations against this move by tens of thousands of Jews, first at Ptolemais on the coast and later at Tiberias, by Lake Galilee. The preoccupation with what the Emperor was trying to impose on them must have made the campaign against the followers of Jesus less of a priority. It was not time to be persecuting Christians when the most precious heritage of their religion was at stake.

Before any statue could be imposed on the Temple, Caligula was assassinated and Claudius, the next Emperor was friendly to the Jews at the beginning of his reign(AD 41). This meant that for a decade or more the Jews reverted to their own factions, divisions and abortive revolutionary movements and left the Followers of Jesus alone.

The Care of the Churches

Just as Peter and John had gone to Samaria to confirm those who believed as a result of Philip's ministries, so Peter, after Saul was sent off to Tarsus, went down towards the coast of the Mediterranean to visit God's people who, lived in Lydda, one day's journey from Jerusalem. This is the area where Philip evangelized after leaving the newly baptized Ethiopian Official (Acts 8:40).

In Lydda he came across a man named Aeneas, who was paralyzed and had not been able to get out of bed for eight years. We do not know if he was a believer or not. We do know that he attracted Peter's special attention. Peter addressed him directly, 'Aeneas,' Peter said to him, 'Jesus the Messiah makes you well. Get up and make your bed.' At once Aeneas got up. This made a huge impression on the locals there and there was a wholesale turning to the Lord, not just in Lydda, but among people who lived in the plain of Sharon just north of the town (Acts 9:32-35).

There is a feeling of normality in the narrative of these events. This one was just like the healing of the cripple in the temple after Pentecost. (Acts 3:1-10) It also had echoes of similar healings by Jesus in Jerusalem, (John 5:1-18) and Capernaum (Mark 2:1-12). We are getting a picture of events that keep on happening with the apostles in these days. Lives were being transformed by the power of the Spirit.

Doing as Jesus did

While Peter was in Lydda, he had a summons that took him down to the sea port of Joppa about three hours journey further on. (Modern Jaffa) There lived a very attractive woman called Dorcas, a disciple, who spent all her time doing good and helping the poor. She made garments for widows who were struggling to make ends meet and was deeply respected for her helpfulness. Tragically, she became ill and died. Relatives and friends washed her body and laid it out in an upstairs room. It sounds like a more spacious house than some, but it is a little strange that they did not proceed to bury her on the same day as we have seen was the custom in Jerusalem (Acts 5:6,10).

The reason for the delay was that they had heard that Peter was at Lydda, a short distance away. They sent two men to request that he come to them without delay. There was expectancy in their actions. Peter got ready and went with them. As soon as he arrived, he was taken to the room upstairs, where the body lay. It was a distressing scene. A number of widows crowded around him crying for their loss. They were at pains to point out that both the undergarments and the coats that they were wearing had been tailored by Dorcas when she was alive. Their gratitude and affection for her were evident in their faces.

Peter had been in this kind of situation before in the early days of following Jesus (Mark 5:35-43). With a calm demeanour, he took charge of the present situation. Peter put them all out of the room, and knelt down and prayed; then he turned to the body and said, 'Tabitha, get up!' She opened her eyes, and when she saw Peter, she sat up. Peter reached over and helped her get up. He had been enabled to do what he had seen Jesus doing, raise a dead person. It must have been awesome and yet, the story moves on without fuss or histrionics of an kind. He called all the believers, including the widows, and presented her alive to them. The news about this spread all over Joppa, and many people believed in the Lord.

The Early Church Norm

These were dramatic events described in a very undramatic way. We are reading about the lives of ordinary believers, in normal homes, who had no claim to fame, doing good as they were able, except that the Lord worked in their lives and others were impressed and believed also. This was how the gospel spread. This is how it can spread today.

I recall listening to a Chinese Church leader in Nanjing in China. He was asked the reason for the phenomenal growth of the churches in China since 1978. He replied that the main reason for it was the lives of the believers. They were reliable workers. They completed their quotas of work without fuss, even if they were sometimes overly demanding. When other people were stressed out to the point of being psychologically damaged by the pressures upon them, the believers visited and prayed with them and many were healed. Even when they had other sicknesses but no medicines were available, the Christians offered to pray for the sick and often they were healed. They were the most reliable and caring people in the deeply stressed society under the cultural revolution and this led to many more people believing in Jesus also.

A Humble Dwelling

Peter did not go back either to Lydda or to Jerusalem. He stayed on for a considerable time in Joppa. Although he was the leading apostle, he chose to lodge with a man called Simon who was a tanner of skins by trade. It is likely that his home was also his place of work. Tanneries are foul smelling places as I recall from having to pass a factory often in my younger days. In strict Jewish society, in addition, tanners were regarded as ceremonially unclean because they were so much in contact with dead bodies and unclean animals. It was a despised trade. If a tanner married without mentioning the fact to his wife, she was permitted to get a divorce.

A tanner's yard must be at least 25 yards from any town. Perhaps in Joppa it was isolated by the seaside where the winds carried the stench out to sea. Yet this is where Peter elected to live for a considerable time. It not only proves how modest were the resources which Peter could command but also that he was learning to rise above prejudice and to recognize the dignity of labour in even the humblest trade. The apostles cultivated no airs and graces!

17

Cornelius: 'Seeking and Finding'

Acts 10:1-11:18

A Seeking Soldier

Cornelius was a Roman officer over 100 men. We can assume a habit of ingrained obedience, great courage, and unflinching loyalty. Since he was a Roman soldier, he belonged to one of the finest armies the world has known. Its deeds of valour went back through an almost unbroken record of success through seven centuries.

The centurions were the backbone of the Roman army. They were of farming peasant stock and came in as foot soldiers. They rose through the ranks and were given their limited command because of their loyalty, commitment and skill as fighting men. When Rome was being corrupted from the top down, the centurions maintained their sterling character for much longer than the generals and higher officers.

When the Roman civil wars ended, about twenty years before the birth of Jesus, Caesar Augustus became the first Roman Emperor. He had far too many soldiers and they had not been paid regularly. He dissolved several forces and made them one army, well paid and supplied. He began the practice of giving to his centurions a piece of land which they could cultivate and develop in semi-retirement and live on for the rest of their lives. This land could be in Italy or in any other of the countries that Rome had occupied. There are two of these retired or semi retired centurions in the New Testament. They are presented in a favourable light. The Jews said about one of them, 'He loves our nation, and has built us a synagogue'. Jesus added his commendation, 'I have not found so great faith, no, not in Israel.' (Luke 7:5,9) Cornelius, is the other. He had chosen to retire in or near the city of Caesarea.

Caesarea was a modern city. Herod the Great built and dedicated it to the Emperor, Augustus Caesar and called it Caesarea after him. It was a spacious sea port and became the seat of government for the Roman province of Judea. It was one of its largest cities, highly cosmopolitan but in which several thousand Jews also lived. There were frequent disturbances between the Jews and the majority non-Jewish population.

Cornelius may have chosen to settle in Caesarea because he was attracted to the Jewish religion. There were many Jews there and it was not far from Jerusalem, the heart of the Jewish faith. He was clearly searching for meaning in life and was attracted by the God whom Jews believed to be the one and only God with a character that could be admired and revered. When he comes into our story, he is still searching, but has made a lot of progress. Nonetheless, he was aware that something was still missing in his life. Cornelius, then, was a man in middle life, 50 plus in age, not from a great family, who had seen service in several countries, and had risen through discipline and merit to his present situation.

A Conscientious Convert

We are told that, he was a religious man and worshipped God (Acts 10:2). This is a technical term, 'God fearer' that describes a person who is almost a full convert to Judaism but has not taken the last and final step of being circumcised. Full converts were called 'proselytes' like Nicolaus, one of the Seven (Acts 6:6). Cornelius was half converted to Judaism.

The main change in 'God-fearers' was that they gave up having anything to do with idols of any kind and sought to worship God alone. After instruction, they attended the synagogue and kept the Sabbath day holy as did the Jews. They followed the Law of Moses as their moral guide and adopted other Jewish customs, like abstaining from eating blood, or food offered to idols and things strangled. They engaged in prayer and, if they were very devout, observed at home some of the Jewish times of prayer in the Temple in Jerusalem. They fasted from food on certain days and they made a regular habit of giving to the poor. In some cases, these, often wealthy converts gave substantially to their local synagogue for building works (Luke 7: 5) and also to the temple in Jerusalem. All of this Cornelius did conscientiously. He was serious about his search for God.

A New Factor

In the years when Cornelius was devoting himself to his search for God and getting to know the faith of the Jews, news started to reach Caesarea about strange events inland. Peter indicated that the basic facts about Jesus of Nazareth were known to him. 'You know of the great event that took place throughout the land of Israel, beginning in Galilee after John preached his message of baptism. You know about Jesus of Nazareth and how God poured out on him the Holy Spirit and power. He went everywhere, doing good and healing all who were under the power of the Devil, for God was with him.' (Acts 10:37-38) We do not know what he made of this information that was filtering through from up country, but we can assume that it would be taken seriously by the kind of person that Cornelius was.

A Harmonious Household

We are told that the whole family worshipped God and shared his search and there is evidence that it was a household where there were good relations between the family and their servants. When he sends servants to find Peter, they are called by a term that means domestic servants and not slaves. It suggests that they were valued and cared for. He takes them into his confidence and briefs them fully about his visit from an angel. When they return they and everyone else in the household is included in the group that Peter is asked to address. He includes also his relatives and even some intimate friends (Acts 10:24). He had a personal attendant, a soldier naturally, but he too shared his superior's religious convictions. He was the one chosen to lead the party to Joppa.

We are not surprised that he was highly respected by the Jewish people. There must have been one sadness in the household. They never had a visit from any of the Jewish friends they made at the synagogue, not even the leaders who had instructed them in the Jewish faith and welcomed them to Sabbath worship.

A Special Messenger

One day during his regular afternoon prayers, Cornelius had a visit from an angel, something very rare indeed. He saw it quite clearly; it had the form of a man with bright shining garments. It spoke his name. He was transfixed with wonder and terror and asked, 'What is it, Sir?'

The answer must have been a wonderful encouragement to him. 'God is pleased with your prayers and your works of charity and is ready to bring you an answer. Jesus had said that God sees people praying, giving or fasting in secret and rewards them, even if no one else sees(Matt.6:4,6). Here it was happening for Cornelius right in the middle of his prayers. The answer, however, was not a revelation, or a gift, or anything immediate. He was given something to do. 'Send some men to Joppa for a certain man whose full name is Simon Peter. He is a guest in the home of a tanner of leather named Simon, who lives by the sea.' The angel went away, just as it had come.

We do not know how that instruction sounded to Cornelius. The house of a tanner was not a very salubrious place even if it was by the sea. It was by the sea, away from the town, so that the sea breezes would waft away the stench of the tanning process. No one very important was likely to be found at that address. But Cornelius was a disciplined soldier who was carrying his discipline into his search for God, so he called two of his house servants and a soldier. He told them what had happened and sent them off to Joppa. (Acts 10:3-8, 30) For him, the next thing was to wait.

There is every evidence that this was a peak experience for Cornelius. His quick despatch of his small party to Joppa, his unusual deference to Peter when he arrived, four days later, his gathering his household and friends in anticipation of Peter's visit and his total readiness to receive whatever Peter said, all indicated that he felt uncommonly privileged by the visit of the angel.

A Sea Change

Cornelius was completely unaware of what was happening to Simon Peter whom he had sent his messengers to invite to Caesarea. He knew nothing of Peter's vision or the words that the Holy Spirit was saying to prepare him for this invitation. It is always difficult to judge precisely when a tide turns and starts to come in. Cornelius did not know that the tide had begun to turn even before Peter arrived. His three servants were the first to know when they were invited to spend the night under the same roof as this same Jewish Peter (Acts 10:23). Perhaps the fact that it was the odoriferous house of Simon the Tanner remotely located by the sea, made it less conspicuous that Peter should give such an invitation. Perhaps Simon the Tanner was not a Jew, although this hardly seems likely, knowing Peter's prejudices. At all events, the tide had begun to turn when Peter chose six other believers to accompany him on this potentially historic journey (Acts 11:12). The party of ten must have been bemused as they travelled the thirty miles to Caesarea.

A Receptive Audience

I would guess that Peter expected to meet Cornelius the Centurion in a face to face encounter. If that is so, imagine his surprise then to arrive and discover the whole household and extended family and selected friends filling the room waiting for him to speak.

Imagine his embarrassment when the sturdy Cornelius, of military bearing, fell at his feet, bowing down before him! What had he come to? Quickly, he put Cornelius at his ease assuring him that he was very much a man like himself and there was no need for such deference as they walked into the building engaged in friendly chat.

He launched in with a comment on the irregularity of his being there at all since he was a Jew and Jews were not allowed by their religion to visit or associate with Gentiles. He explained, 'God has shown me that I must not consider any person ritually unclean or defiled. And so when you sent for me, I came without any objection. I ask you, then, why did you send for me?'

This was already revolutionary to Cornelius. No doubt by this time his three servants had let him and everyone else they talked to know about staying the night with Peter. So, on cue, Cornelius launched into the story of the angel visit. His family and servants already knew about this, but it must have heightened the expectation of any in the gathering who were hearing it for the first time. He was not exaggerating when he finished up by saying, 'Now we are all here in the presence of God, waiting to hear anything that the Lord has instructed you to say' (Acts 10:24-33).

Most of Peter's speech was standard stuff as we have seen earlier. It is the new note at the beginning that was significant both for Cornelius, his friends and family and also for us. 'I now realize that it is true that God treats everyone on the same basis. Those who worship him and do what is right are acceptable to him, no matter what race they belong to.' Everything else took on a new light with that start. Jesus the Messiah was opening a door not just for the Jews, but for them and the world that no one had ever dreamed would be opened.

Suddenly it was Pentecost all over again. The Holy Spirit came down on the whole gathering and they were speaking in tongues, repenting and praising God just as it had happened in the Temple. What to do? The obvious thing was to get down to the sea and have this fine household baptized in an impromptu event that must have raised many eyebrows (Acts 10:34-48).

The Opening of a Door

Cornelius disappears from the story, never to be mentioned again. Peter has still a few appearances to make and in one of them he uses Cornelius's story to good effect when the policy of the church about the Gentiles was being decided (Acts 15:7-9).

The message of Cornelius is that when we seek for God with our whole heart, we shall surely find him, for he is also looking for us. He wants to find us and will press angels and visions and providences into his mission to find those whose hearts are warm towards him. In countries where believers are a tiny minority, there are an increasing number of stories coming out where by visions and dreams and angelic experiences, Jesus is calling individuals and families to himself.

18

Peter

A Tale of Two Homes

Acts 10:1-11:18. 15:7-11

The Original Home

What do we know about Peter? His given
name was Simon. His family came originally
from Bethsaida at the head of the Sea of Galilee.
His father's name was Jonas or John. In Jesus'
time, Simon's home was in Capernaum,
further to the west. He was married and lived
there, oddly enough, with his mother-in-law.
Simon had inherited from his father some traits
of character that Jesus did not want in his
disciples. When Jesus looked at him he said,
'You are Simon, son of John, but you will be
called Peter' (John 1:42). He was a chip off the
old block! There were characteristics that
Simon had inherited from his father John and
brought from his old home, that Jesus could
see would not fit with his being a disciple of
his.

One of the latest psychologists to emphasize the influence on the rest of our lives of what we absorb from our homes is Howard Gardner of Harvard. He talks about the 'five year old world view' and maintains that most of our worldview is formed before we go to school. What is more significant is that he shows that we retain this world view in many of its parts for the rest of our lives. One of these ingrained features that we imbibe is the sense of who are our people and who are not – the sense of 'us and them'. This is the seat of racism, tribalism, class, caste and all the things that grow into deep seated prejudices.

This Simon who became Peter was a Jew, a very strict Jew. He had a tendency to be bigoted, boastful, bombastic, arrogant, competitive and volatile emotionally. He had strong opinions and he spoke them out. He could use foul language at times. After three years with Jesus, and after going through the experience of the cross, resurrection and the coming of the Holy Spirit, there was a marked change in Peter. He became number one in the new church in Jerusalem. There was, however, one very important change that he had to face. He still was exclusively a Jew ten years after Pentecost.

There is a bit of word play with the names 'Simon' and 'Peter' in the New Testament. It is most noticeable in John's gospel, the writer who tells us in his first chapter about Jesus saying, 'You are Simon son of John but you will be called Peter' (John 1:42). In his last chapter he records the encounter where three times Jesus calls him Simon son of John and questions him about his love for himself. It is interesting that the only time Peter is called Simon in Acts is in the Cornelius story. It is the angel and Cornelius, at the angel's prompting, who use this name. I take this to mean that here is yet another instance where Peter needs to face up to the fact that his five year old worldview, imbibed from his home, needs to be changed. The issue this time is his exclusive Jewishness.

The Home of Revelation

Peter was now far from home in Galilee. He was in Joppa at the coast and had been lodging with Simon the Tanner for some time. It was not a great place to live with the stench from the skins and the process of tanning. Fortunately it was by the Mediterranean sea, separated a bit from the town. Not surprisingly Peter went on to the rooftop overlooking the sea to pray. Like many of us, when he started to pray he felt hungry and asked for some food to be prepared for him downstairs in the house. While he was waiting for it he 'fell into a trance' (AV) or 'had a vision.' He saw heaven opened and something coming down that looked like a large sheet being lowered by its four corners to the earth. In it were all kinds of animals, reptiles, and wild birds. It must have been a very large something like a sheet if it contained a selection of the live animals that were forbidden to Jews to eat.

A voice said to him, 'Get up, Peter; kill and eat!' I do not know if it was the surprise of it all, or because he was operating out of his unconscious but Peter reverted to type and spoke just as he had at Caesarea Philippi (Matt.16:22) and in the upper room (Mark 14:29) 'Certainly not, Lord!' This time it was, 'I have never eaten anything ritually unclean or defiled.' This is his third never! We should always be careful; when we find ourselves saying 'Never!' and, 'Always!' These are often words from our five year old worldview. Peter's lifelong eating habits were getting in the way of his obedience to the heavenly voice. The voice spoke to him again, 'Do not consider anything unclean that God has declared clean.' This happened three times, the same vision, the same response. Then 'the thing' was taken back up into heaven.

While Peter was wondering about the meaning of this vision, the men sent by Cornelius, a Roman Officer in Caesarea, had learnt where Simon's house was, and were now standing in front of the gate. They called out and asked, 'Is there a guest here by the name of Simon Peter?' Peter was still trying to understand what the vision meant, when the Spirit said, 'Listen! Three men are here looking for you. So get ready and go down, and do not hesitate to go with them, for I have sent them.' So Peter went down and, sure enough, the men were there. He said to them, 'I am the man you are looking for. Why have you come?' They were from Caesarea about eight or nine kilometres further north on the coast.

They replied, 'The centurion Cornelius sent us. He is a good man who worships God and is highly respected by all the Jewish people. An angel of God told him to invite you to his house, so that he could hear what you have to say.' Peter invited the men in and persuaded them to spend the night there. We do not know the ethnic background of the three men. One of them, a soldier, was likely to be Roman. The other two servants could have been of any ethnic group. Caesarea was a very cosmopolitan city and Jews did not like to work for Romans. The fact that these three were invited to stay the night was the first hint that something was happening to Peter. Three non Jews spent the night in the house of Simon the Tanner with Peter in the same house. In this hospitality to Gentile strangers, Peter had taken a first step to discovering what the will of the Lord was.

The Home of New Relationships

The next day Peter got ready and went with them; six believers from Joppa went along with him. The following day he arrived in Caesarea, where Cornelius was waiting for him, together with relatives and close friends that he had invited. Apologetically, Peter said to them, 'You yourselves know very well that a Jew is not allowed by his religion to visit or associate with Gentiles.' He was saying that they should not really be there. 'But,' he went on, 'God has shown me that I must not consider any person ritually unclean or defiled. And so when you sent for me, I came without any objection. I ask you, then, why did you send for me?'

Cornelius described how an angel had told him to send for Peter. In turn Peter explained the gospel to them all and the Holy Spirit came on them and they became believers and were baptized. Peter and his six friends stayed with them for a few days before going back to Jerusalem.

Is food and hospitality so important? It was here, because on Peter's attitude to it depended the reception of the gospel by non Jews. Food can be important but the more important thing is whether you will eat it in someone else's house or have them to eat in your house. The good news of Jesus grew more in homes than in any other way. Before AD320, there is archaeological evidence of only two church buildings and they were big houses modified and could only hold about seventy people. That was the period of the most rapid growth of the church in history and they had no church buildings. The most natural way for the gospel to spread was in the homes of welcoming and caring Christians. It is still true that potentially, the closest frontier to the non Christian world is in the homes of Christians.

The Roots of Prejudice

This was a radical new departure for the Church, perhaps the most significant since Pentecost. What can we learn from it for the twenty-first century. How did Peter come to have these prejudices? He tells us.

He held to ideas and practices that had the force of law that were not laws. 'You know that a Jew is not allowed by his religion to visit or associate with Gentiles.' (Acts 10:28). This was a custom that had the force of a law for the Jews in the world of the New Testament. It was not in any sense biblical. It was an inference from their food laws and the ban on intermarriage that was enforced at particular times.

The most recognized of these are traditional practices about which we say, 'We have always done it this way.' New spiritual movements also fall into this 'legalism'. In the East African Revival there were matters nowhere written, that had the force of law. Sleeveless dresses, the parting or the dressing of the hair, a ban on beards, the idea of courtship, smoking, drinking alcohol, dancing, partying etc. In each case there was an element of scriptural argument about the matter and for some people in some circumstances they were good rules. Yet by having the force of law, they bred a legalism that stereotyped Christian behaviour and made it a caricature that repels. It became a cultural obstacle to the gospel.

Peter had little or no contact with the excluded people. Acts 10:28 shows that up until this point Peter had not associated with Gentiles. He had no contact with them. He judged them from afar, by hearsay, or by stories told of them. This was in stark contrast to Jesus. He refused to bow to the cultural ideas of his day. People shunned Samaritans, Gentiles, Pharisees, street girls, corrupt civil servants. He had contact with them all. He was accepting of them, was attractive to them and they came to him. One of the key discoveries of the Willowcreek Church is that the key to successful growth in a church is for the members to have non Christian friends. The trouble with Christians in the west is that very few of us have non Christian friends.

He had reason to fear criticism from his own community. As soon as he went back to Jerusalem he was faced with severe criticism for his actions (Acts 11:2-3). He had to be prepared to stand his ground and not be cowed by the attitudes of censorious people.

The New Family
How can we divest ourselves of our cultural straightjackets. It is not just differences of ethnicity or race. It happens between generations. Education can be a barrier. Our income and life style tends also to affect the people we meet with naturally. There are also different subcultures even in different denominations. Some of it is just snobbery.

It helps if we recognize that we are all in this transition from being 'Simon, son of John,' to a new 'Peter'. Peter says it. 'You know what was paid to set you free from the worthless manner of life handed down by your ancestors. It was not something that can be destroyed, such as silver or gold; it was the costly sacrifice of Christ, who was like a lamb without defect or flaw... For through the living and eternal word of God you have been born again as the children of a parent who is immortal, not mortal. . . He has given us . . . promises . . . so that we. . . may come to share the divine nature.' (1 Pet.1:18,23, 2 Pet.1:4) The transition from our own family to the family of God is no easier than the transition from our own family to the new family we form with our partner in marriage.

There has been talk in UK about our police and other public bodies being 'institutionally' racist. It would be better if we recognized that coming from the families we come from, we are all 'constitutionally' racist. We start out with the prejudices of our family and upbringing. These are deeply engrained. They can last a lifetime. One of the functions of the Christian gospel is to give us a new birth that enables us to draw on the divine nature as children of God. This has to be worked at and it would be better if we all realized it and made a conscious effort to check all our instinctive behaviour and change it if it denies the gospel of a God who loves the world.

Involve others with you in your Change

It is a little thing, but Peter took with him six believers from Joppa to Caesarea. They all heard what Peter said. They all stayed there for some days enjoying the hospitality of Cornelius. They were there as witnesses of what actually happened. In fact it is only when he is defending his action to the other apostles that we learn that there actually were six fellow believers with him. He makes the point that they 'all went into the house of Cornelius' (Acts 11:12). Peter did not leave himself exposed as the only one who defied custom in this matter.

Old Teaching

When Jesus was on earth, Peter had actually asked a question about what makes a person unclean. Jesus told him it was what came out of a person that made him unclean, rather than what went into him in the way of food (Matt.15:15). Peter seems to have forgotten this. Yet now when he was confronted with a situation where the teaching began to fit, the

Holy Spirit brought it to his remembrance. We all have a battery of truths in our heads that are still waiting to be recalled and acted on.

Act Promptly

This was one occasion where Peter's impulsiveness was the right thing. As soon as his vision was over and he heard that the men were at the door, he went down, greeted them, welcomed them into the house for the night and travelled the next day to meet Cornelius. Prompt obedience to what God is saying about our relationships will make us more loving and more like him. Four times in Peter's life God told him not to be afraid, so he was in the same boat as we are.

Be True to the Gospel

It is interesting to look at the talk Peter gave to Cornelius and his household. It is a classic statement of the gospel with nothing omitted. It is just like Peter's earlier sermons with the addition about God not having favourites at the beginning. Cornelius was already a God-fearer or a person who had been converted to the Jewish faith and knew the OT background. Paul still preaches the death and resurrection of Jesus the Messiah and the fact that he will be the judge of the living and the dead who demands repentance and faith as the only way into his kingdom. There is no change to his message even if there is a vast change in his attitude.

Come Back after Lapses

Peter would not be Peter without his messing it up sometime. When Peter came to Antioch, he had been eating with the Gentile brothers and sisters. But after some men who had been sent by James arrived Peter drew back and would not eat with the Gentiles, because he was afraid of those who were in favour of circumcising them. Some other Jewish brothers and sisters also started acting like cowards along with Peter; and even Barnabas was swept along by their cowardly action. Paul saw that they were not walking a straight path in line with the truth of the gospel, He said to Peter in front of them all, 'You are a Jew, yet you have been living like a Gentile, not like a Jew. How, then, can you try to force Gentiles to live like Jews?' (Gal 2: 11-14) The tone of his letters shows that Peter returned to the stance he had learned with such difficulty in the house of Simon the Tanner.

Long Term Consequences

This was a close shave, but Peter came through. The consequences if he had resisted this sanctifying work of the Holy Spirit are almost unthinkable. We see it in India, where the caste system still prevails in many Christian Churches. Christian parents are not ready to agree to their sons or daughters marrying into a different caste. It affects their willingness for their offspring to marry new converts and it even spills over into the situation where sometimes their denomination operates like a caste for them. There is no saying how much more rapidly the church in India might have grown if they had experienced in the early days the kind of encounter that Peter had with Cornelius.

19

Herod Agrippa I

God is Greater

Acts 12:1-25

Four Herods

Four Herods invade the story of the New Testament, all with a malignant influence. Herod the Great massacred the infants around Bethlehem when Jesus was born. (*Characters around the Cradle,* Chapters 1 and 11) Herod Antipas beheaded John the Baptist and tries Jesus (*Characters around the Cross*, Chapter 9).

Herod Agrippa I executed the apostle James and imprisoned Peter and is the subject of this chapter. Herod Agrippa II tried Paul before he was sent to Rome.

Up until this time, the early followers of Jesus clashed mainly with the Jewish religious authorities, the High Priest and the Sadducees. Now that they are not just a Jerusalem phenomenon but have spread to Judea, Galilee, Samaria, and the coast, (Acts 9:31) they begin to get the adverse attention of the political authorities. Herod Agrippa is the first of these and his are very political acts.

The Road to Kingship

He is called 'King' Herod (Acts 12:1) and it was by a very round about road that he became king. He was born in 10BC. His grandfather, Herod the Great, murdered his father. It was not a good start in life. His mother then took him to Rome where he was brought up in all the luxuries and intrigues of the Imperial court. He was pro-Roman to a fault. He became a special friend of Drusus, the Emperor Tiberius's son whom he used for his own advantage. Drusus died and Herod lost the favour of the Emperor. He had to leave Rome, and the next fourteen years of his life were a roller coaster of varying fortunes. At one time he thought of committing suicide. He ran up enormous debts and borrowed from new creditors to pay off the old ones even more generously, in a spiral of dependency. Sadly, he spoke out of turn and expressed his hope that the Emperor would die soon and let his living son, Gaius, ascend the throne. A slave overheard this and reported it to Tiberius and Herod was sent to prison in the most abject conditions.

Tiberius did die earlier than expected (AD37) and Gaius, his son, who became Caligula, not only got Herod out of prison, but gave him a gold chain equal in weight to the iron chain with which he had been bound. He also gave him the territories of his brothers, Philip and Lysanias and the title 'king'. In AD38 he visited his new possessions, but in AD39 he was back in Rome. He was responsible for the banishment of Herod Antipas in AD39, and was given his territory in addition to what he already had. The death of Caligula (AD41) and the accession of the Emperor Claudius gave him an opportunity of winning the goodwill of the latter and he received Judea and Samaria in addition to his other possessions, and ruled therefore over all the territory of his grandfather.

Herod, the Man Pleaser
The leading feature of his three year reign was his almost manic cultivation of the Jews, in spite of his having been pro-Roman all his previous life. He showed extreme regard for Jewish customs. He offered all the fitting sacrifices in the temple. He dedicated in the temple the golden chain which he had received from Gaius. He constantly lived in Jerusalem, and preferred it. He kept the laws of his

country exactly. He lived a life of the strictest
holiness, and allowed no day to pass without
offering the sacrifice. He used his political
influence to preach Judaism. When he
betrothed his daughter, Drusilla, to Epiphanes,
son of Antiochus, king of Commagene, he
made him undertake to be circumcised. His
arrest and execution of the apostle, James, was
part of his obsessive desire to curry favour with
the Jewish religious authorities.

The Victim

James is only mentioned in Acts here and in
the list of apostles at the beginning where he
is moved to the place after his brother John,
instead of before him. James was not
prominent in the story of the Jerusalem
church, only featuring incognito where 'the
apostles' as a group are mentioned. Maybe that
was why Herod selected him to try out his
new policy of harassing the followers of Jesus
of Nazareth. Or it could have been a hint from
the High Priest. The family of James and John
was known to the High Priest (John 18:15) and
he may have felt it a special embarrassment to
have a friend of the family among the followers
of Jesus, whom he had crucified. The fact that
he was beheaded indicates that this was a
political execution. It paid off. The Jews were

pleased and Herod was emboldened to take it one step further. He had the leader, Peter, arrested – by accident or design – just before the Festival of Unleavened Bread. His plan was to have him brought out and publicly tried after Passover when the maximum number of pilgrims would be in Jerusalem. That would have been highly symbolic, for Jesus had been crucified at the same festival season about fourteen years before. In view of a previous escape from prison he ordered the strictest security this time(Acts 12:1-4).

Not so Fast

Herod had not counted on God. His plans seemed to be maturing well through the days of the festivals and every day he must have breathed a sigh of relief that his security measures were still intact. On the night before the planned trial, however, the whole situation changed dramatically.

Peter was sleeping between two guards. He was tied with two chains, and there were guards on duty at the prison gate. Suddenly an angel of the Lord stood there, and a light shone in the cell. The angel shook Peter by the shoulder, woke him up, and said, 'Hurry! Get up!' At once the chains fell off Peter's hands. Then the angel said, 'Fasten your belt and put on your sandals.' Peter did so, and the angel said, 'Put your cloak round you and come with me.' Peter followed him out of the prison, not knowing, however, if what the angel was doing was real; he thought he was seeing a vision. They passed by the first guard post and then the second, and came at last to the iron gate leading into the city. The gate opened for them by itself, and they went out. They walked down a street, and suddenly the angel left Peter.

At this point Peter came to his senses and realized what had happened to him. Naturally, he saw it as divine intervention. He said, 'Now I know that it is really true! The Lord sent his angel to rescue me from Herod's power and from everything the Jewish people expected to happen.' Herod had been nonplussed and he was free. He visited the praying believers, let them know what had happened and then disappeared to we know not where (Acts 12:17).

Consternation
When morning came, there was tremendous confusion among the guards. What had happened to Peter? Herod gave orders to search for him, but they could not find him. Herod was so disconcerted at his plans being foiled that he had the guards summarily executed for

something they had not had anything to do with. Uncharacteristically, he stormed out of Jerusalem, his much preferred residence, and went down to Caesarea at the coast, the chief city of the province.

There was a remarkable parallel in the life of Sadhu Sundar Singh when he was preaching in Tibet (*Mrs. Parker* p.64ff). ' He was arrested and arraigned before the head Lama on the charge of entering the country and preaching the Gospel of Christ. He was found guilty, and amidst a crowd of evil-disposed persons he was led away to the place of execution. The two favourite forms of capital punishment were being sewn up in a wet yak skin and put out in the sun until death ends the torment, or being cast in the depth of a dry well, the top being firmly fastened over the head of the culprit. The latter was chosen for the Sadhu.

When he arrived at the place he was stripped of his clothes and cast into the dark depths of this ghastly charnel-house with such violence that his right arm was injured. He alighted on a mass of human bones and rotting flesh. Any death seemed preferable to this. Wherever he laid his hands they met putrid flesh, while the odour almost poisoned him. In the words of his Saviour he cried. 'Why hast thou forsaken me?' Day passed into night, making no change

in the darkness of this awful place and bringing
no relief by sleep. Without food or even water
the hours grew into days and Sundar felt he
could not last much longer.

On the third night, just when he had been
crying to God in prayer, he heard a grating
sound overhead. Some one was opening the
locked lid of his dismal prison. He heard the
key turned and the rattle of the iron covering
as it was drawn away. Then a voice reached
him from the top of the well, telling him to
take hold of the rope that was being let down
for his rescue. As the rope reached him he
grasped it with all his remaining strength, and
was strongly, but gently pulled up from the
evil place into the fresh air above.

Arriving at the top of the well the lid was
drawn over again and locked. When he looked
round, his deliverer was nowhere to be seen,
but the pain in his arm was gone and the clear
air filled him with new life. All that the Sadhu
felt able to do was to praise God for His
wonderful deliverance, and when morning
came he struggled back to the town, where he
rested until he was able to start preaching again.

His return to the city and his old work was
cause for a great commotion. The news was
quickly taken to the Lama that the man they
all thought dead was alive and preaching again.

The Sadhu was again arrested and brought to the judgment seat of the Lama, and being questioned as to what had happened, he told the story of his marvellous escape. The Lama was greatly angered, declaring that some one must have secured the key and gone to his rescue; but when search was made for the key and it was found on his own girdle, he was speechless with amazement and fear. He then ordered Sundar to leave the city and get away as far as possible, lest his powerful God should bring some untold disaster upon himself and his people.'

Nemesis

The mystified Herod had plenty other business to attend to in Caesarea that took his mind off the Jerusalem disaster. Josephus, the Jewish historian gives us the details. There was a dispute about food supplies between Herod and the people of Tyre and Sidon further north. It was a time of famine (Acts 11:28). There were also celebrations in a public-stadium in honour of the Emperor Claudius and his successful return from a campaign in Britain. On a chosen day Herod put on his royal robes, sat on his throne, and made a speech to the people. 'It isn't a man speaking, but a god!' they shouted. At once the angel of the Lord struck Herod down, because he did not give honour to God. He was eaten by worms and died (Acts 12:21-23)

Herod had not reckoned on God. He had spent his life manipulating and using people for his own advantage, always able to think up some new scheme by which someone could get him out of his latest scrape. All unknown to himself, it was affecting his health and he was struck down in the most public place.

He joined Nebuchadnezzar (Dan.4:31-37) and Belshazzar (Dan.5:25-31) and made up the trio of public figures in the Bible whose soul was required of them for dereliction of their acknowledgment of God.

The Danger of 'Good Works'

In his time in Judea as king, Herod was full of good works. He was assiduous in keeping the law and performing religious ceremonies. The Jews loved it. It was in such contrast to earlier rulers that Rome had imposed on them. What they did not know was that this was all 'policy' to win their support and affection. It had an ulterior motive that was purely personal. Herod was doing his good works for the earthly salvation of getting people to like him and help him. It was the pattern of his whole life. He was constantly using and manipulating people. He was buying people with his generous loans and gifts. He found as a boy that it worked with Drusus, the Emperor's son and others, no doubt his mother included and it became the story of his life.

He was self deceived. Alternately he saw himself as the paragon of generosity or the one whose friends were letting him down. He believed his own story. He also deceived others as such people do. Con men tell a great story and even believe it, but the root of it all is inveterate self interest. It is here that we need to hear the word from Paul, 'Do not deceive yourselves; no one makes a fool of God. People will reap exactly what they sow. If they sow in the field of their natural desires, from it they will gather the harvest of death; if they sow in the field of the Spirit, from the Spirit they will gather the harvest of eternal life' (Gal.6:7).

I once attended a barbecue for about a hundred people who had all been on visits at different times to Third World countries. Many of them said it had changed their lives. I pressed one of them to be more specific and tell me how it had changed her life. She was a TV producer. She was reluctant to speak but eventually she said this. 'All my life I have never known a relationship where I was not asking myself, 'What can this person do for me?' Then I went to Africa and met people who had very little material wealth. Yet they were ready to share their best with us who they would never see again. That showed me there was another way to live. That other way is the way of the gospel.

Alas! There are many professed followers of Jesus who are still like my TV producer friend before her visit to Africa. They want to use people. They cannot think of a relationship that is not somehow going to benefit them. They are like Herod and only God knows. But that is enough.

20

Mary and Rhoda

Church and Home

Acts 12:6-16

Two women, Mary the mother of John Mark, and Rhoda, give us a little glimpse into the Jewish Christian home in the early church (Acts 12:12).

The Home Owner
If Mary was the mother of John Mark, she was a relative, probably the sister of Barnabas (Col.4:10). Barnabas, alias Joseph, had been a land owner in Cyprus who sold land there and gave the proceeds to the common purse in the early days of the church (Acts 4:36-37). Thereafter he supported himself with the work of his own hands (1Cor.9:6). Mary, on the other hand, owned a house and was a resident of Jerusalem. She did not sell the house like Barnabas, but opened it up for the use of the apostles and other disciples. We would like to

know more about this property owning woman. Was she a wife, a widow or had she never married? Was the house her share of the family inheritance, or left to her by a deceased husband?

Scholars speculate that Mary's house contained the upper room where Jesus and the apostles celebrated the last supper; (Luke 22:12) where the disciples met between the Resurrection and the Ascension; (John 20:19) where the 120 met while waiting for the coming of the Holy Spirit; (Acts1:13) and to which Peter and John returned after their trial and prayed (Acts 4:23-31). There is no evidence to prove this but it helps us to imagine the role that homes played in these early days of the church to know they had to find all these places in a city that was not home territory to any of the apostles.

It seems it was a house of a considerable size considering the meetings for which it was used. The phrase, 'the church which is in your house' occurs several times in Paul's letters and draws attention to the fact that the homes of those who owned them were the principal places where the church met for the three centuries of its most rapid growth. Homes and meetings in them for prayer and Bible study in Korea were the secret of the growth of what became the largest church in the world in the 1960-70s, Yoiddo Full Gospel Church.

In Addis Ababa in the 1980s when the Mennonite Meserete Kristos Church lost its pastors and its buildings, they resorted to doing church quietly in the homes of the Christians. They grew in ten years time from 5,000 to 50,000 members. These examples have given rise to the strategy of the 'cell church' in many places in the West, but the key factor is the readiness of those who own homes to use them for the Kingdom. This is particularly true when one of the major movements of our time are the Diasporas of people from Africa, Asia and Latin America to the West. The welcome they receive may well be the main factor determining the growth of the churches in this century. By hospitality to the stranger in our homes we shall stand or fall.

The Mother

Mary was the mother of John Mark. Within days of this incident her son was co-opted by his uncle Barnabas and taken off to Antioch where he became part of their mission team to Cyprus (Acts 13:5). Mark travelled first with Barnabas and Saul and later with Peter and ultimately became the writer of the gospel that bears his name. Mary would have every reason to be anxious about how her son would fare in these early days in these exacting circumstances. In fact he did not do very well and was soon back in Jerusalem and not covered with glory (Acts 13:13). He picked himself up, apparently and went on to be the reporter of Peter's preaching which must have made his mother proud.

Mary gave her son back to the Lord for the work of his kingdom and saw little of him for many years, because of his travels. This is a call that still comes to parents. Our children are the Lord's more than they are ours. My wife and I both had mothers who were widows, who lent us to the Lord for the work of the kingdom in Africa. They missed out on us and their grandchildren and made other sacrifices yet could not have been more supportive than they were. There will be a 'well done!' for them and those like them in the days when the books are opened in the world to come.

The Hostess

Recently they had all been shocked and saddened when James the apostle was abruptly executed by Herod. Then Peter had been arrested and had been kept under very close guard during the festival to await public trial when the Passover was finished. After the

Apostle's earlier embarrassing escape from prison, under the High Priest (Acts 5:17-27). Herod was taking no chances and had sixteen men on round the clock security duty to ensure Peter did not get away this time (Acts12:4). It was a desperately worrying time. They were in danger of losing their leader and spokesperson. They prayed earnestly and constantly for his safety and release. In desperation they decided to pray right through the night before the fatal day. Mary said they could come and use her place.

Their faith was not very great as the sequel shows. The lesson of it is that we should make our homes places of prayer not just for us but for and with others. The promise is there for the twos and threes to pray and be even more assured that God will answer (Matt.18:19-20). Mary allowed the disciples to assemble for prayer all through the night before Peter was due to be tried in public before Herod, the king.

The Mistress
Mary had servants. One of them was Rhoda. In the middle of the night when they were praying for Peter's safety and release, there was a loud knocking on the outer door. Rhoda was the servant who went to see who it was. She

must have been apprehensive. Indeed they all must have been fearful of this knocking in the night in the climate that obtained at the time. Who were they coming to arrest now?

As she crossed the courtyard toward the outer door she recognized Peter's voice. She was so happy that she ran back in without opening the door, and announced that Peter was standing outside. The people inside thought she was mad and said so. Rhoda stuck to her story and they started looking for other explanations, like it was his ghost or an angel or some other apparition.

They were in the grip of what I call obligatory doubt. When you cannot imagine a rational solution to your prayer, you are slow to believe that anything will happen. Descartes was the French philosopher who made doubt obligatory in every sphere where there was no rational explanation. This is now pervasive throughout the societies of the West. It is manifest most noticeably in our media, both press, radio and TV. Argue against, or put the opposite side to everything that is said or that is claimed to have happened. Stir up conflict in the mind of the audience, for that is the way to get ratings and thence profits.

The story of those who prayed in the house of Mary the mother of John Mark says that we should be praying even when we are not sure that anything will happen. We need to leave what Bob Pearce used to call 'God room'. He has more ways of answering than we can imagine as this little company of anxious believers were about to discover. Peter kept banging on the door, they went to investigate and sure enough it was Peter. When they saw him, they were amazed.

Rhoda was clearly not just a servant. She shared her mistress's concerns about Peter and obviously knew his voice well. There was clearly a good relationship between mistress and servant. This became a key factor in a valid witness for early Christians (Col.3:22-4:1). In the Kingdom, there are no little people. When the door was opened to Peter, there he was in his street clothes. He did not go in for any length of time.

Peter quietened their excitement and explained to them how the Lord had brought him out of prison. This time his angel had not told him to go back to the Temple and preach again. The situation had changed drastically. Peter left a message, 'Tell this to James and the rest of the believers,' he said; then he left and went somewhere else. Where he went we do not know. He went into hiding and it was better that no one should know. It implies that

Peter judged that it was not safe for him to be around and that he had better encourage James to assume the leadership of the Jerusalem church which we know he did.

The Church in the Home

There are further advantages of using homes to 'do' church. It increases the opportunity for voluntary service and opens the doors of service more widely to lay people and especially to believing women.

21

James

Drinking the Cup

Acts 12:1-2

'About this time King Herod began to persecute some members of the church. He had James, the brother of John, put to death by the sword.'

It seems that the sole reason why Luke told us about the death of James is to show that he died a martyr's death and that he drank that cup first of all the twelve apostles. Even in doing so he has to mention the central factor in James's life. He was the brother of John.

A Brother Problem

James is never mentioned in the New Testament without it mentioning his brother John also. All the writers invariably couple him with his brother. Jesus invited them on the same day to follow him and he would make them fishers of men. They left **their** father,

Zebedee, and their nets to become his disciples
(Luke 5:10). With Peter, they formed a kind
of inner circle of three whom Jesus took with
him on special occasions. Peter, James and John
went with Jesus into the house of Jairus when
Jesus brought his daughter back to life (Luke
8:51). They went up on the mountain with
Jesus when he spoke with Moses and Elijah
and was transfigured before them (Luke 9:28).
The three went further into the garden of
Gethsemane with Jesus when he prayed in
agony before his death (Mark 14:33).

With five others, they went fishing when
they thought it was all over after Jesus' death
(John 21:2). Even when Herod executed him,
and he was separated from his dear brother by
death, Luke still calls him 'James, the brother
of John.' They often mention John on his own,
but never James. They nearly always mention
James first. It is 'James and John.' It is never
'John and James'! This shows that James was
the older of the two. Thank God for brothers
and sisters and all they have been to us and
done for us. Yet we know that sometimes there
can be sibling problems.

We do not know how many years there
were between James and John. Those who
study these things, say that the older child is
'dethroned' when a baby brother is born. No

doubt this happened to James when John was born. Yet, we know that James and John became very close. The older brother tagged along with his brighter, more attractive, and ultimately more famous younger brother. Yet he hung in there. They seemed inseparable.

It can go different ways when you have two siblings. They can each go their own way as in the story of the prodigal son and the elder brother. They can even become enemies like Cain and Abel. When they stick together, it can be because the older one feels he needs to be there to protect the younger. Equally it can be because they just don't want to miss out on the better chances that the brighter sibling gets. It can just be an expression of family solidarity. It seems that this may have been the reason because they both had:

A Mother Problem

Matthew tells the story differently. 'Then the mother of Zebedee's sons came to Jesus with her sons and kneeling down asked a favour of him.' They had a mother who was very ambitious for her sons. Zebedee, their father was a more prosperous fisherman. He could afford to employ servants. The family were also friendly with the high priest in Jerusalem (John 18:16). His wife was called Salome and she seems to have been a sister of Mary the mother of Jesus (Matt.27:56, Mark 15:40, 16:1, John 19:25). When James and John followed Jesus, it meant leaving their nets and their father and the hired servants. It seems that Zebedee made no objection. It also appears that Salome may not have taken it so well. When she could, she went along with her sons. She was one of the women who helped to support Jesus out of their own means (Luke 8: 1-3). Maybe she was the organizer! She certainly is with them when going up to Jerusalem (Mark 10:32). She was present at the crucifixion and went to the tomb to help embalm the body of Christ. Our story gives the impression that she was there looking after her sons' interests and was not unsuccessful in imparting her ambition to her sons.

Three stories give us the flavour of this woman's family. First, Jesus gives them the nickname, the 'MacThunders' or sons of Thunder (Mark 3:17). So we are not surprised when James and John want to call fire down from heaven to destroy the people in a village in Samaria, who did not welcome Jesus. Just before that John had tried to stop a man driving out demons in the name of Jesus, because he was not one of their party (Luke 9:49,54). If Jesus gave us a nickname, what would it be?

Where did this vindictive streak in James and John come from, if not from their mother? I think this is why we know the mother's name. We know Jonas was Peter's father's name. We know another apostle's father for he was James the son of Alphaeus. We know no other apostle's mothers or their names. The gospels name people when they still knew them in the church when the gospel was written. Hearing Matthew just calling her 'the mother of Zebedee's children' (Matt.20:20) without a name is so strange. She seems to personify something.

Alexander Whyte has a classic paragraph or two that are worth quoting, slightly modified. "'Leave it to me, my sons," said Salome, "leave it to me. Do not be in any doubt about it. It will all come right. I am not his mother's sister for nothing; and I have not followed him about all this time and ministered to him out of my substance for nothing. Blood is thicker than water, and you, my sons will see that it is so. You were disciples as soon as any of the rest of them. And you got management experience in our fishing business. Leave it to me! Who is Andrew? Who is that unstable Peter? Who is their father? Who is their mother that they should presume to be princes over my sons? It will never be! Leave it to me my sons; leave it to me!'"

'Then came to him the mother of Zebedee's children with her sons, worshipping him and desiring a certain thing of him. He said to her, "What wilt thou?" She saith unto him, "Grant that my two sons may sit, one on thy right hand and the other on the left in Thy Kingdom."'

Well done, Salome! Well done! As long as this gospel is preached, this splendid impudence of thine shall be told of thee! Let the sons of all the other mothers in Israel sit, stand or lie as they like. Only, let my two sons sit high above them all and have their feet on the necks of the ten.

Had Salome's presumption been less magnificent, our Lord would have been very angry at her. But the absolute sublimity of her selfishness completely overcame him. He had met with nothing like it. He is overcome with the splendid shamelessness of Salome's request. Her cold-blooded cruelty to himself also pierced his heart as with a spear. This is Monday and he is to be betrayed on Thursday and crucified on Friday. All the same, Salome went on plotting and counterplotting for a throne for her two sons. The thrones only existed in her own stupid and selfish heart. It was the sight of all this that made our Lord's rising anger turn to an infinite pity, till he said to her two sons: Are you able to drink of my cup and be baptized with my Baptism? What do you think the two insane men said? They actually said, 'We are able!' In such sin had their mother conceived them, in such stupidity of mind, in such hopeless selfishness, combined with such hard hearted presumption. They had a Brother problem and a Mother problem. Now they had:

A New Problem

When Jesus asked them if they could drink the cup that he would drink and be baptized with the baptism that he was about to suffer, he presented them with a new challenge. It meant, 'Could they die to the things that up to that point they held dear? Would they break with the kind of person that their family had conditioned them to be?'

If we pick up on the concept of the 'five-year-old world view', (See p. 204) James and John had become the MacThunders from the backwash of their mother's dominant style in the household and the strong sense of family solidarity that she inculcated. She was all for her children achieving great things, no matter who got in the way. They instinctively behaved like that even after they became disciples of Jesus. So do we. We carry into our lives as Christians all the instincts that our families have bred in us.

Now they were being asked if they could die to that and become more the sons of their heavenly father than children of their earthly parents. There were good things in their family tradition. There always are. It was just that the basic selfishness and unthinking family solidarity did not fit with their being children of God who loves everyone alike.

This is what being born again is about. 'That which is born of the flesh is flesh,' said Jesus. In my case that is Houston flesh. There is no other kind. Yours is (put in your family name) flesh. This is not enough to get us into the Kingdom of God. We need to be born again. It is the Spirit that does this. We are born of the spirit to change what needs to be changed in our inheritance from our own family .

The Responses

How did James and John react to Jesus' challenge? Not immediately! Immediately they caused a furore in the other ten apostles by their naked ambition. It took Jesus a while to calm them down and get over the teaching they all needed to hear. They were not to be like others looking after number one. They were to serve and not be served and ready to give up their lives as he was about to give his.

Even after this telling off, James was among those who forsook Jesus and fled when they arrested and took him to be crucified. But he is still around after Jesus dies, when seven of them decide to go back to their fishing. He is there on the shore and hears Jesus recommissioning Peter to be a shepherd of his people (John 21). It looks as though he had changed when he was part of 'the one accord' that they came to have in the upper room when the Holy Spirit was given to them. So he stays around.

Then the only thing more that we hear is that Herod selected him for execution. This is when we learn that he had renounced the old self that his family had made him. This is when we know that he had made his choice and joined the company of Martyrs who did not count their lives dear to themselves. James MacThunder had become James MacMartyr.

The word for 'martyr' in Greek is also the word for 'witness'. We do not hear one word out of James in the whole New Testament. Jesus calls and includes the reticent among his disciples. He has room for the clannish and the vindictive but they do not stay like that. James's witness to Jesus was in being ready to give up his life for him. In the end, few of the twelve apostles died in their beds. James was the first to die for Christ.

John changed too. In Acts he is the silent companion of Peter in his early preaching and healing. It almost feels as though this were an apprenticeship in public ministry. The younger MacThunder became the Apostle of Love, writer of the gospel and the letters. Significantly, his last word was that the younger Christians should keep themselves from idols.

Some of us are older. We are senior citizens. As we grow older, we sometimes begin to recognize how unthinking and unbending we have been. When we get the perspective of being mothers-in-law and fathers-in-law, or grandparents, or uncles and aunts, we see things in ourselves that we were not conscious of before. It is not too late to change. It can happen without us telling anyone. But it will not happen without others noticing it.

Death before Death

We have some dying to do every day (1 Cor.15:31). James was confronted with his need to die to the family stranglehold on his character just before the crucifixion (Mark 10:38). He responded positively at the time and showed how genuine he was in that, when he kneeled before Herod's executioner. The more we die along the way to what dishonours Jesus in our lives and temperaments, the less of a hurdle death will be when we face it.

So let us pray the Collect for St. James's day.

Merciful God, we pray that as your holy Apostle Saint James left his father and all that he had and obeyed the calling of your Son Jesus Christ even to death, so may we forsake every selfish desire and be ready always to answer your call, through Jesus Christ our Lord. AMEN.

22

James, the Lord's Brother

The Local and the Global

Acts 12:17, 15:13-21, 21:17-26, Gal.1:18-19, 2:1-14

Changes in Jerusalem

Peter effectively disappears from Acts at chapter 12:17 after his dramatic release from Herod's clutches. Later, he has only one walk-on part at the Council at Jerusalem, where he tells again, without names, his experience in the home of Cornelius (Acts 10-11:18).

There are two men called James in Acts 12. James, one of the twelve apostles, is beheaded by Herod at the beginning (Acts12:1-2). Peter asks for the news of his escape to be conveyed to another James (Acts12:17). With James the Apostle dead and Peter gone, this other James became the leader of the Church in Jerusalem. Paul identifies him for us as 'James, the Lord's brother' (Gal.1:19).

The Late Convert

Jesus had four brothers and at least two sisters (Mark 6:3). The oldest brother was James. We get this information in a paragraph that describes the scepticism that Jesus met with in his home town of Nazareth. Mark has already indicated that his own family shared this local scepticism.They thought Jesus was unbalanced in his mind and tried to restrain him (Mark 3:21,31-35).

We have then to imagine how James and the others managed to cope with Jesus their older brother as they grew up in Nazareth before anyone except Mary and Joseph had any hint that he would be the long expected Messiah. From all the legends it is clear that James grew up a very strict religious young Jew. He became known as 'the just' like his father, Joseph before him (Matt.1:19). It seems as though Jesus was the sunny character and James more serious and gloomy, not an unusual combination in any family.

The crunch came, however, when Jesus began his public ministry. By this time it is assumed that Joseph had died. The question of Jesus being the Messiah arose. James would have none of it and neither would his mother, Mary, or the rest of the family. It stayed like that, as far as we know, right up to the crucifixion. Paul tells us that after he was raised from death, Jesus appeared to James (1 Cor. 15:7) and we know that the whole family had joined the believers before Pentecost (Acts 1:14). James was a late convert.

The Ethnic Shake Up

So long as all the believers were Jews, there was comparative harmony. When non-Jews like the Samaritans and the household of Cornelius found faith and joined the church, controversy was inevitable (Acts 11:1-3). This naturally coincided with much more travel outside Jerusalem and even beyond the borders of Judea towards Damascus and Antioch, as the apostles pursued their various missions. Add the fact that Herod began specifically to target apostles and mark them out for elimination, and you can see that new leadership arrangements were inevitable. Since the church in Jerusalem were almost entirely Jews in a strident Jewish population, it was politic for any new leaders to have a Jewish face and not rock the boat with innovation. In these circumstances, James the Lord's brother came into his own and seemed a natural choice to lead the Jerusalem church.

It is worth noting that when communities are homogeneous and made up of one kind of people in a relatively settled population, the question of racial or tribal integration of the churches may not be an issue. The increasingly nationalistic fervour in Palestine in the years AD50-70 meant than non-Jews were tiny, insignificant minorities.

Similarly, when Third World countries which were mainly rural were evangelized, it was natural that churches were made up of people from single tribes. Comity arrangements were made between missions to limit themselves to agreed geographical and ethnographic areas. This reinforced what would have been the trend anyway. Once urbanization took off and people migrated in thousands to the towns and cities, the ethnic composition of churches became a serious issue and a real problem. This is still in process of being worked out in continents like Africa.

Control from the Centre?

The first big issue that James had to handle was whether non Jewish believers had to conform to Jewish practices like circumcision and matters of ceremonial law. Trouble-

making believers began to dog the footsteps of
Paul and his teams and tried to insist that all
the new converts had to be circumcised. This
was proving very disruptive and so Paul and
Barnabas decided to go to Jerusalem to get
agreement about the matter.

It was a very contentious meeting that went
on for a long time. There was input from all
sides. There was a 'party of the Pharisees' who
took the extreme dogmatic position that
everyone had to be circumcised (Acts 15:5).
Peter retold his experience in the household
of Cornelius in Caesarea and the conclusions
they came to at that time. He argued for an
outright exemption from Jewish practices for
Gentile believers (Acts 15:7-11). There was a
lot of very convincing anecdotal evidence from
Paul and Barnabas (Acts 15:12).

James, then, who seemed to be presiding,
backed up completely from scripture and
experience what Peter, Paul and Barnabas had
been arguing (Acts 15:13-19). The argument
seemed to be going all their way, when James
proposed a middle position. He suggested four
items where non Jews should be asked to
conform. One was moral. They should abstain
from sexual immorality. Two were about
kosher food and one was a social restriction
from eating food that had been offered to idols.

He argued that these would not be unexpected 'for the Law of Moses has been read for a very long time in the synagogues every Sabbath, and his words are preached in every town.' (Acts15:20-21) It carried the day and a letter was written and representatives chosen to communicate the message.

I am impressed by the fact that in the early church it is not important who presides at meetings. Peter handled the meeting to elect the successor to Judas (Acts 1:15-26). He disciplined Ananias and Sapphira (Acts 5:1-11). All the apostles worked out the election of the Seven (Acts 6:1-6). Here we can just about conclude that James was in the chair. I am also impressed by the way that the whole church were encouraged to participate in some part of the decision making process. James did not rule on the four requirements. They were proposed and agreed (Acts 15:22).

Pillar or Broken Reed

As they implemented this new ruling back in Antioch, they ran into trouble emanating from James. Paul in Jerusalem had called James along with Peter and John, a pillar of the church (Gal.2:9). Now, however, when Jews and non Jews were mixing freely and happily including Peter and Barnabas, some men sent from James arrived and the atmosphere changed completely. They all retreated into their culinary ghettos and ate separately. James, if he could be judged by his messengers, was less like a pillar and more like a broken reed. If you use a reed as a stick to walk with, it is liable to break and pierce your hand (Isa.36:6GNB). The problem was not yet completely resolved but they all persevered in a mutually supporting spirit.

Paul took one big initiative. He organized, over three years, a collection from the churches in Greece and what we call Turkey and took it to Jerusalem for the relief of poor believers in Judea – it was the wrong way round. The mother church should have been helping the daughter churches. Paul was apprehensive about how his gesture of solidarity would be accepted (Rom.15:31). When he arrived, he went the next day to see James. We never do find out how the money was received.

In the view of James, there was a crisis that had to be dealt with first. Paul and James gave each other basic but encouraging reports of how their different churches were faring (Acts 21:17-20). James then reported on the rumour mill that had been undermining Paul's Jewish credentials. Paul, he thought, was in real personal danger. He had thought up an elaborate damage limitation exercise that was intended to restore Paul's good standing in the eyes of the conservative Jews. It had to do with a rather remote Jewish custom. It did not get the chance to succeed. Paul was mobbed by his enemies, taken into custody by the Romans, and eventually sent to Rome for trial (Acts 21:27-26:32).

This is the last we hear of James, the Lord's brother in Acts. There was no attempt made in Jerusalem, that we read of, either to pray or negotiate for Paul's release. Just silence. He spent two years in prison in Caesarea at the coast with not a believer in sight except Luke. We know he is there because he writes in the first person, 'we' as he described what happened. If there had been attempts, surely Luke, being on the spot, would have told us about them.

The Elevation of the Local

The Jerusalem church, the earliest church was engulfed in a sea of insane nationalism and barely survived. James's attempts at accommodation with the Jewish population and leadership back fired. Only with difficulty did a remnant survive the destruction of Jerusalem in AD70 and begin to grow again in the second century AD. The centres of gravity of the church moved successively to Antioch Ephesus, Alexandria and Rome.

If, as many believe, the Letter of James in the New Testament was written by James, the Lord's brother, we get a stern but beautiful picture of how Jewish Christians like him lived and talked about their faith. We are eternally grateful for this but even there we realize that its focus was on the Jewish Dispersion in many lands rather than on their homeland of Palestine. It is evidence, if we needed any more, that they may have made a mistake in elevating their local context and culture to stand aloof from the great outward movement that the church of Jesus Christ had to be, if God loved the world. The world had to know. The world had to hear in language that it could understand within each of its many varied contexts.

It is a lesson that was later repeated in North Africa when the gospel stayed in the language of the expatriate rulers and did not penetrate the culture of the Berbers. When the Muslim armies came, such a church was no match for Koran based conviction, backed by the sword. It is a lesson that needs to be heeded today where the local considerations of backward looking churches are put above the longer term opportunities that accommodation to other cultures and later generations will bring.

23

Jesus' Tears for Jerusalem
Luke 19:41-44

There is something incredibly poignant about the last conversation Jesus had with his disciples before the Ascension (Acts1:6-8). The disciples ask, 'Will you at this time give the kingdom back to Israel?' They did not realize that in only forty years the Jewish state would cease to exist. Yet, Jesus told them, for the second time, to begin their witnessing in Jerusalem. In forty years, there would be virtually no church in Jerusalem at all.

The Love Affair with Jerusalem
The Jews had a kind of love affair with the city of Jerusalem and its temple, ever since David captured and founded it (2 Sam.5:6-10). This devotion to Jerusalem is reflected in several Psalms (Psalm 48, 84, 87, etc.) and echoed in our hymns based on them like 'Jerusalem the golden...' and 'Glorious things of thee are spoken.'

Jesus seemed to share that attachment to the Holy City. References to the Temple and the city are like landmarks in the progress of his life. Before he was conceived, Zechariah had his vision in the Temple of the birth of John the Baptist, the forerunner of Messiah (Luke 1:5-22). In infancy he was presented in the Temple to the sounds of dire prophecy from the saintly Simeon (Luke 2:22-38). As a boy, he held his own in debate with the teachers in the Temple when he should have been on the way home to Nazareth (Luke 2:41-52). The pinnacle of the Temple was even the locus of his temptation from the Devil to seek notoriety (Luke 4:9-12).

Disillusionment

Disillusionment set in, however. By the time he began his public ministry, in his thirties, his zeal for the house of the Lord moved him to try to cleanse it from its mercenary practices (John 2:17). He taught in the Temple every year when he went up for the festivals. Often he was not well received by the authorities and the atmosphere became increasingly adversarial.

On several occasions and with great sorrow he began to predict the destruction of Jerusalem and its Temple within a generation.

The reasons he gave for this were:

- They kept killing the prophets, and stoning the messengers God sent them (Luke 13:34a).
- They did not know what was needed for peace (Luke 19:42).
- They did not recognize the time God came to save them (Luke 19:44).
- Particularly, they turned away from the love and protection that Jesus tried to bring them (Luke 13:34b).

He signalled to them that this catastrophe would be preceded by unimaginable persecution (Mark 13:9-13). They should be ready to flee to the mountains when it all began to happen (Luke 21:21). Jesus is still intensely conscious of this coming tragedy even on his way to be crucified. He spoke of it to women who were sympathizing with him in his plight. 'Don't cry for me, but for yourselves and your children. For the days are coming when people will say, "How lucky are the women who never had children, who never bore babies, who never nursed them!" That will be the time when people will say to the mountains, "Fall on us!" and to the hills, "Hide us!" For if such things as these are done when the wood is green, what will happen when it is dry?' (Luke 23:27-31).

The predictions about Jerusalem seem mostly to have been made only to the apostles. We get no indication that they became general knowledge in the Jerusalem church. In the event, however, everything matched closely what Jesus had foretold. There was the rampant outcrop of Messianism with one after another claiming to be the anointed one. The furious persecution is illustrated by what Josephus the Jewish historian says happened to James the brother of Jesus.

James's Popularity and Martyrdom

There are hints in the literature that James, Jesus' brother was hugely popular even with non believers and led a highly successful mission to the Palestinian Jews. There might be a hint of this in the report James gave to Paul about his work. 'Brother Paul, you can see how many thousands of Jews have become believers and how devoted they are to the Law' (Acts 21:20). The word he uses is the word for tens of thousands, but translators tend to play that down. Sources say that the Jewish priests began to fear that the whole populace would be converted.

In these circumstances a jumped up High Priest decided to take pre-emptive action. 'During the interval between the death of the

Roman Governor, Festus (AD62) and the arrival of his successor Albinus, the high priest Ananas the younger, being of a rash and daring spirit, and inclined like the Sadducees in general to severity in punishing, brought to trial James, the brother of Jesus, who is called the Christ, and some others before the court of the Sanhedrin, and, having charged them with breaking the laws, delivered them over to be stoned' (Jos. Ant.20.9.1). Two authors also cite Josephus as ascribing the miseries of the later terrible siege to divine vengeance for the murder of James.

The War and the Siege

Soon after that, the Jews declared their independence and the war started. And what a war and a siege it was – perhaps the worst the world has ever known. The narrative of Josephus shows that there were never more horror frenzies, unspeakable degradations, and overwhelming miseries than in the siege of Jerusalem. There was never any prophecy more closely, more terribly, more overwhelmingly fulfilled than that of Christ. Men went about in the disguise of women with swords concealed under their gay robes. Priests, struck by darts from the upper court of the Temple, fell slain beside their own sacrifices. The blood of all sorts of dead carcases, priests, strangers, profane, stood in lakes of blood in the holy courts. The corpses themselves lay in piles and mounds on the very altar slopes. The fires fed luxuriously on cedar-work overlaid with gold. Friend and foe were trampled to death on the gleaming mosaics in promiscuous carnage. Priests, swollen with hunger, leapt madly into the devouring flames, till at last those flames had done their work. What had been the Temple of Jerusalem, the beautiful and holy House of God, was a heap of ghastly ruin, where the burning embers were half-slaked in pools of gore.

Many saw their fellows crucified in jest, 'some one way, and some another,' till 'room was wanting for the crosses, and crosses for the carcases'. 600,000 dead bodies were carried out of the gates. Friends fought madly for grass and nettles and the refuse of the drains. A miserable mother in the pangs of famine, devoured her own child. People were sold for slaves in such multitudes that at last none would buy them. Streets ran with crimson streams, and the 'fire of burning houses was quenched in the blood of their defenders'. Their young sons were sold in hundreds, or exposed in the amphitheatres to the sword of the gladiator or the fury of the lion. At last, 'since the people were now slain, the Holy House burnt down, and the city in flames, there was nothing farther left for the enemy to do.' In that awful siege it is believed that 1,100,000 men perished, beside the 97,000 who were carried captive, and most of whom perished subsequently in the arena or the mine.

The Christians Escape

Four years before the end, the Christians had a revelation that led them to escape and flee to a town called Pella on the other side of the Jordan, twenty miles south of the Sea of Galilee. This was regarded as treachery and increased the Jewish hostility to the Christians in the Diaspora. In Pella the remnant of the Jerusalem church survived. They were demoralized and divided into sects. The originals were called the Nazarenes, the name used for believers by hostile Jews in Jerusalem before they left Jerusalem. (Acts 24:5) They were just like the rest of the believers we see in the Acts except that they observed the Law of Moses including circumcision. Two groups broke away from them. The Jacobites or followers of James were not too keen on Paul. The Ebionites were more problematical. They rejected the virgin birth and believed that Jesus was adopted as the Son of God at his baptism.

They were more insistent on observing the Law, especially circumcision, rejected the mission to the Gentiles and avoided contact with foreigners.

Reprisals

Roman reprisals for the rebellion came on the Jews in two stages. After the siege, all land was confiscated. A Jewish Poll Tax was imposed on all Jews throughout the Empire that caused hardship, especially to poorer large families. Temple worship was forbidden and there were no High Priests, no Sanhedrin or Great Council or any ruling class. With the extinction of their metropolis, their cultural, political and economic structure was shattered.

This was deeply resented and led to massive Jewish rebellions in Egypt, Cyprus and Cyrene in AD115. Then in AD132 there was a second great rebellion in Palestine itself led by Bar Kochba. Again they were defeated and decimated. This time, Hadrian the Emperor had Jerusalem renamed Aelia Capitolina and rebuilt it as a pagan city with temples to Jupiter (power) and Venus (sex). Jews were excluded from the city and its surrounding territory. The country was renamed Syria-Palestina and the name Judea forgotten. Circumcision was forbidden throughout the Empire at least for the lifetime of Hadrian.

The Jerusalem Church

It is interesting to look back at the characters
mentioned in the early chapters of Acts from
the perspective of the destruction of Jerusalem.
Three had died as martyrs, Stephen, James, the
apostle and James the Lord's brother. Some,
of course would already have died in the
natural course of things. The lame man was
forty when he was healed and this was thirty
five years later, so he could have gone to his
reward. Philip, we already know had moved
to Caesarea and Peter had been martyred in
Rome. Some, we have some reason to believe,
ended their lives elsewhere, like John in
Ephesus, Andrew is said to have been crucified
on an X shaped cross in Patrae in Achaia;
Thomas worked in Parthia, Persia or India;
Matthias is associated with Ethiopia and
Barnabas with Alexandria. Was it at this time
they left? Did Matthew move to Pella with the
refugees who escaped there and who made his
gospel their gospel of choice. But there are
intriguing gaps. Did many survive the ordeal?
Did the remainder of 'The Seven' keep
ministering to the destitute to the last? Was
the house of Mary the mother of John Mark
and mistress of the servant Rhoda demolished
in the razing of the city to the ground? Or was
hers the house in Mount Zion in which we

hear that a small congregation was allowed to lie low?

In spite of the wars, a miniscule Christian presence seems to have survived in Jerusalem or to have recommenced due to the return of some after the war. The historian Eusebius names the bishops in Rome after James but only until the Bar Kochba rebellion. There was, however, little authority left in the Jerusalem Church in stark contrast to its position at the Council of Jerusalem in Acts 15. The Greek Orthodox Church in Jerusalem claims to go back to Pentecost, but they are a Gentile (Arab) Church. The Jerusalem church virtually goes out of the picture for three hundred years. After AD324, the Emperor Constantine and his wife began to build the first ever Christian church buildings in Jerusalem. They built the earliest version of the Church of the Holy Sepulchre which pilgrims and tourists still visit today.

All of this helps us to understand the tears Jesus shed over Jerusalem and the irony that must have been in his soul when he told the apostles to begin there. Paul had earlier asked, 'When the Jews stumbled, did they fall to their ruin? By no means! Because they sinned, salvation has come to the Gentiles to make the Jews jealous of them. The sin of the Jews brought rich blessings to the world and their spiritual poverty brought rich blessings to the Gentiles. Then how much greater the blessings will be when the complete number of the Jews is included!' (Rom.11:11-12) The same Jesus who wept over Jerusalem, himself saw an end in sight, however far off. 'The heathen will trample over Jerusalem until their time is up' (Luke 21:24). Strangely interwoven with his predictions about Jerusalem was the affirmation, 'This good news of the kingdom will be preached through all the world for a witness to all mankind and then the end will come' (Matt.24:14).

Today

We live almost two millennia later, in a time when the blessings of the gospel have come to billions of us Gentiles in every known country in the world. There has been a new State of Israel since 1948. It is still riven with factions and assailed by terrorists but has within it a Messianic Jewish presence in addition to the historic Orthodox, Catholic and Protestant Churches. This community is not large. There are just over ninety congregations of varying size and about 5,000 believers. In the last ten years it has begun to grow a little while the historic churches are declining steadily from emigration.

Some Jewish and Arab believers are working hard at reconciliation and promoting mutual understanding of each other in the midst of incredible tension and violence. Groups of young Jewish and Arab believers go annually out to the bleakness of the desert to live with each other for short periods in primitive surroundings. They get the chance to express their feelings of prejudice and frustration and sometimes hate to each other and be listened to. When they return home, they remain in contact by phone, E-mail, letter and visits as they are able. The organization, Musalaha, has begun similar mutual education ministries with church leaders from both communities. These are signs of hope in a desperate situation.

The Jerusalem March

In October 1999, before the 2000-2002 conflict began, there was an annual March in Jerusalem hosted and organized by the Jerusalem Municipality. Banks, Factories, Businesses, Scout groups, Premises, etc., sent their representatives to participate. The Messianic movement also sent a group to march.

About a hundred participants donned T-shirts and marched with Israeli Messianic believers the length of Jaffa Road in Jerusalem during the Feast of Tabernacles celebrations.

They danced and openly praised the Messiah Jesus in song in the streets of Jerusalem. The spirit of celebration was expressed in the lovely work of the dancers and tambourinists. They were received with applause for most of the way. It brought together believers from all over the country. They learned more about each another, heard news of how God is working within the congregations across the country, prayed for one another and gave thanks to the Father for the Family of believers in Israel. Many thousands of viewers were witnesses to the fact that the movement was alive and well.

Because the movement was growing, opposition was there also. The anti-Messianic Yad L'Achim organization heard about their messianic participation and organized their own event parallel to what was planned by the believers. Forty-three orthodox extremists gathered from around the country to harass the believers, as they participated in the march. They walked among the rows of the believers and tried to persuade some of them to drop out and study at one of the many schools they have. They shouted 'traitors' and curses almost the whole way of the march. The city sent March Marshals to accompany the believers almost the entire route of the march. The marshals evicted those who became too violent.

One of the marchers said, 'Despite the harassment, it is hard to describe adequately the joy involved when marching through the streets of Jerusalem, singing praises and blessing the Lord before all the multitudes. Sometimes it seems incredible that we could publicly proclaim the praises of Messiah Yeshua, all to the applause of the inhabitants of the City! In some small way, it brought to mind the account of the entry of Jesus into Jerusalem two thousand years ago with the hosannas from the rejoicing crowds in Jerusalem.' It was a sign that Jesus' tears for theIU city will, in the long haul, be effective in bringing peace to Jerusalem.

Preaching on Bible Characters

The aims in preaching on Bible Characters

1. Short term:

1. To get the attention of the congregation.

2. To get across a truth of the gospel.

3. To tell it in their language (Family Talk/ Popular Psychology).

4. To start post service conversations.

2. Long Term:

1. To fill in people's knowledge of the Bible story. (Biblical Literacy) like painting by numbers.

2. To give them help with everyday problems, relationships and conduct and a means of talking about these things with others.

Tips on how to do it from scratch

1. Do your own basic work on the text. There is a lot more there than we have noticed, so,

this means going over it in detail to get all the elements of the 'story'. (One way of doing this is to write out the passage taking a new line for each phrase or thought.) Pay attention to the relationships of the person to their family, parents, brothers, sisters, children, and to others in the story. Note the answers to the questions, Where? How far? When? How long? Who? What actually happened in what order?

2. Check all the other references to the person in a Bible Concordance and see what that search yields in the way of background or additional detail.

3. Look up details in a Bible Dictionary.

4. Consult the commentaries for what they say about the person, not so much about the text.

3. Use your imagination! Try to experience and tell the story from the point of view of the main characters in the story.

4. Let it fall into episodes or chapters that will be easy to follow and that build up to one or two main points.

5. Think of illustrations from your own experiences or from biographies, books, magazines or newspapers that you have read.

6. Do a detailed outline or write it out in full but....

7. Tell it as a story. (*Story Telling: A Practical Guide* by Lance Pierson S.U.)

8. One tip on using a character from this book. You need to contextualize what is in the chapter to the place, the time, the people and the occasion when you are to preach it. This usually means:

   1. Reworking how you open and close the sermon to fit the occasion and audience.

   2. Omitting sections that do not apply or would be strange to your audience.

   3. Substituting or adding new illustrations that would speak to your audience.

Other books in the 'Character Studies' series by Tom Houston

Characters Around The

CRADLE

This excellent book makes the Passion come alive
Joel Edwards

Tom Houston

Characters around the Cradle
witnesses to the greatest story ever told
Tom Houston

Tom Houston looks at a great story with a great cast. The political forces of Caesar Augustus, Herod and the travellers from the east, the religious establishment in Zechariah, Elizabeth, Anna and Simeon, The outcast prophet - John the Baptist, the ordinary people - Mary, Joseph and the shepherds and also the Gospellers - Matthew and Luke.

Nativity scenes will never be the same again. Christmas always stirs the imagination, but Tom Houston stirs the readers with reflections from the real biblical characters who surrounded the birth of Jesus ...A lively read that warms the heart.
Chris Wright, International Ministry Director, The Langham Partnership International

Read Characters Around the Cradle and Christmas will live for you in a new way. Perhaps as never before you will realize that the Christmas story was a real happening that can make a difference in your real life today!
Leighton Ford, President, Leighton Ford Ministries

Familiar with the Christmas story? Maybe. But we can miss the extraordinary human drama that surrounds the most remarkable event this world has yet witnessed ...marvel at the way personal details as well as great political movements all combine to demonstrate God's sovereign control..
Jonathan Lamb, Associate General Secretary and head of Bible Ministries, IFES

Tom grabs hold of the characters that he paints, he dissects them, he examines them, and he puts them back together again with a clarity of thought that makes them spring to life. **Dr. Clive Calver**

ISBN 1 85792 7559

Characters Around The

CROSS

This excellent book makes the Passion come alive.
Joel Edwards

Tom Houston

Characters Around The Cross
Tom Houston

In this updated and expanded version of the popular original, Tom Houston brings to life each of the characters involved in the death of Jesus on the cross. He provides us with insights into the historical context of each character and encourages us to imagine the impact that their encounter with Jesus would have had on their lives.

...accurate exposition, lively illustration and contemporary application...

David Coffey, General Secretary of the Baptist Union of Great Britain

After reading the book, I was forced to ask, which of the characters of the cross looks most like me?

Gordon MacDonald, author

This excellent book makes the Passion come alive by opening up the lives of the people we thought we knew so well.

Joel Edwards, General Director Evangelical Alliance UK

I highly recommend it to you, and I plan to draw richly from it in my future Lenten preaching!

John Huffman, St Andrews Presbyterian Church, Newport Beach, Ca

Beautifully written and attractively presented, this book takes the reader to the only place where God will meet us – at the front of the Cross. There we find ourselves confronted by Judas, by Herod and Pontius Pilate, by Mary Magdalene, Nicodemus and others, with a startling vividness that compels us to take sides.

Richard Bewes, Rector of All Souls Church, London

ISBN 1 85792 743 5

Christian Focus Publications
publishes books for all ages

Our mission statement –

STAYING FAITHFUL

In dependence upon God we seek to help make His infallible word, the Bible, relevant. Our aim is to ensure that the Lord Jesus Christ is presented as the only hope to obtain forgiveness of sin, live a useful life and look forward to heaven with Him.

REACHING OUT

Christ's last command requires us to reach out to our world with His gospel. We seek to help fulfill that by publishing books that point people towards Jesus and help them to develop a Christ-like maturity. We aim to equip all levels of readers for life, work, ministry and mission.

Books in our adult range are published in three imprints.

Christian Focus contains popular works including biographies, commentaries, basic doctrine, and Christian living. Our children's books are also published in this imprint.

Mentor focuses on books written at a level suitable for Bible College and seminary students, pastors, and other serious readers. The imprint includes commentaries, doctrinal studies, examination of current issues, and church history.

Christian Heritage contains classic writings from the past.

For a free catalogue of all our titles, please write to

Christian Focus Publications, Ltd
Geanies House, Fearn,
Ross-shire, IV20 1TW, Scotland, United Kingdom
info@christianfocus.com